# AMERICA ARISE and AWAKE

RAMESH SHARMA

authorHOUSE®

*AuthorHouse™*
*1663 Liberty Drive*
*Bloomington, IN 47403*
*www.authorhouse.com*
*Phone: 1 (800) 839-8640*

*Published by AuthorHouse  07/24/2018*

*ISBN: 978-1-5462-5151-4 (sc)*
*ISBN: 978-1-5462-5150-7 (hc)*
*ISBN: 978-1-5462-5149-1 (e)*

*Library of Congress Control Number: 2018908299*

*Print information available on the last page.*

# CONTENTS

Mea Culpa ......................................................................................xv

1.   America Arise And Awake!.......................................................... 1
2.   Émigré ......................................................................................... 53
3.   An Ossified Mirage.................................................................... 55
4.   God Flees The Temple ............................................................... 58
5.   Cruel Irony ................................................................................ 60
6.   He Was Nowhere .......................................................................61
7.   The World Ceases to Exist ........................................................ 62
8.   Visiting A Temple ...................................................................... 63
9.   Ambition.................................................................................... 65
10.  Homosapiens............................................................................. 66
11.  It Owes Its Existence To Me ..................................................... 67
12.  My Tears .................................................................................... 68
13.  Death Is Not Always Ominous ................................................. 70
14.  Beauty Of Nature ...................................................................... 71
15.  My Shadow ................................................................................ 73
16.  Conjugal Bliss ........................................................................... 75
17.  Frightening Cacophony............................................................. 76
18.  About To Be Born...................................................................... 77
19.  I Cannot Find Myself................................................................. 78
20.  I Wonder ................................................................................... 79
21.  I Am Lifting The Universe......................................................... 80
22.  I Have Been Crying And Crying................................................ 81
23.  I Often Feel Like Rummaging ................................................... 82
24.  O My Beloved Motherland! ...................................................... 83
25.  Revolution................................................................................. 84
26.  Tender Longing.......................................................................... 85
27.  What Can Be More Powerful? .................................................. 86
28.  Shallow, Shallow, Shallow ....................................................... 87

29. O Tyrants Of The World! ............................................. 88

30. How Can You Imagine? ............................................. 89

31. O Callous Murderer Of Damascus ............................... 90

32. Bugs and Germs ....................................................... 91

33. What An Irony, Indeed! ............................................. 92

34. Just Be Free And Liberated ......................................... 94

35. Come Out The Chrysalis ............................................ 96

36. Try Not To Wean Me Away ......................................... 97

37. You Are The True Religion ......................................... 98

38. Let Me See .............................................................. 99

39. I Am Above Them All ............................................... 100

40. Vincit Omnia Veritas ................................................ 101

41. Pyongyang Is Desperate ............................................ 102

42. A Wizened Flower .................................................... 103

43. I Don't Want .......................................................... 104

44. Thirteen Years Ago .................................................. 105

45. O My Fellow Beings! ................................................ 107

46. Portrait Of Time ...................................................... 108

47. I Felt Like Crying Again ............................................ 109

48. 'Resist Not Evil' ...................................................... 110

49. I Will Be Looking Forward ......................................... 111

50. I Am Nothing .......................................................... 112

51. God Bless America! .................................................. 113

52. Definition Of My Life ............................................... 115

53. An Eternal Ritual ..................................................... 119

54. Cruel Realities of Destiny .......................................... 120

55. State Of The State ..................................................... 121

56. I Often Question Myself ............................................ 123

57. How Dare You …? .................................................... 124

58. Just Create Something ............................................... 125

59. May I Expect You ..................................................... 126

60. I Propound The Religion of Mass And Energy .................. 127

61. O Star Spangled Banner! ............................................ 128

62. I Am Really Confused ............................................... 129

63. Cause And Effect Unto Myself .................................... 130

64. Solar Eclipse .......................................................... 131

| | | |
|---|---|---|
| 65. | Agony | 132 |
| 66. | Nature Intoxicated | 133 |
| 67. | A Splendid Confluence | 136 |
| 68. | Is It Mere An Illusion? | 137 |
| 69. | I Am The Supreme Deity | 138 |
| 70. | Arise, Awake! | 139 |
| 71. | Ask | 140 |
| 72. | Sole Source of Love | 141 |
| 73. | The Spirit Will Reign Supreme | 142 |
| 74. | O Millennials! | 143 |
| 75. | How Beautiful This World Is! | 144 |
| 76. | Thirst For Pouring Myself Out | 145 |
| 77. | I Am Enthralled | 146 |
| 78. | What A Bizarre Contortion! | 147 |
| 79. | How Can I Reduce Myself? | 148 |
| 80. | Roar Like A Lion | 149 |
| 81. | Knock On The Door Of Your Heart | 150 |
| 82. | O America, I Salute Thee! | 151 |
| 83. | How Blessed Thou Art! | 160 |
| 84. | Why Not Find Some Better Alternative? | 161 |
| 85. | Give Them A Death Kiss | 163 |
| 86. | Something Appears Amiss, My Friend | 164 |
| 87. | What Really Matters Is Truth | 165 |
| 88. | Time Is Always Nonchalant | 166 |
| 89. | How Can You Succumb? | 167 |
| 90. | Ramesh, Hurry Up! | 168 |
| 91. | Ethereal Divinity | 169 |
| 92. | Better To Be An Apostate | 170 |
| 93. | Why We Fail To Heed | 171 |
| 94. | Faith's Deadpan | 172 |
| 95. | Beauty And Ugliness | 173 |
| 96. | How Shall I Define? | 174 |
| 97. | The Moment I Savor | 175 |
| 98. | Why Can't You Tell Your Devotees? | 176 |
| 99. | He Is Here | 177 |
| 100. | Tornado And The Mountain | 178 |

101. I Am Deeply Touched ................................................ 180
102. Destiny Of Time ...................................................... 181
103. Your Destination Beckons You ................................. 182
104. I Don't Want To Evanesce ....................................... 183
105. Don't Get Confused ................................................. 184
106. Be Free And Enjoy Life ........................................... 185
107. How Dare You Expect Me? ...................................... 186
108. I Am Engaged ......................................................... 187
109. How Can I Lay Claim? ............................................ 188
110. I Am Singularity ...................................................... 189
111. With Solitude .......................................................... 190
112. Science Asked .......................................................... 193
113. Workers Of The World Arise And Awake! .............. 194
114. I Was Left Intrigued ................................................ 195
115. Life Is A Haiku ........................................................ 196
116. How Can I Believe? .................................................. 197
117. I Want To Share ...................................................... 198
118. My Dear Bard, I Will Certainly Come ..................... 199
119. Let Me Revel ........................................................... 203
120. Sometimes I Inhale Poignancy ............................... 204
121. Busy, Busy, Busy ..................................................... 205
122. Atrocity Of Time ..................................................... 206
123. Cats Catch Mice ...................................................... 207
124. With A Courtesan .................................................... 208
125. I Don't Want To Cry ............................................... 209
126. Forced To Dissolve .................................................. 210
127. Enemy Has Yet To Be Identified ............................. 211
128. Enjoying Illusion ..................................................... 212
129. I Was Dissolving ..................................................... 213
130. I Want To Forget ..................................................... 214
131. If I Ever Dream Of .................................................. 215
132. Love ......................................................................... 216
133. Poem of Nature ....................................................... 217
134. Milk ........................................................................ 218
135. We Are Mummies ................................................... 219
136. I Had Had A Dream ................................................ 220

137. Sun In Search Of A New Bride .................................................. 221
138. Still A Nightmare.................................................................. 222
139. But There Was No Response.................................................. 223
140. Perhaps My Life Is Not Happy With Me............................... 225
141. Nowhere Could You Be Seen .............................................. 226
142. May I Have Your Permission?............................................... 227
143. Musings ............................................................................... 228
144. Most Beautiful Poem ........................................................... 230
145. I Am Polity ...........................................................................231
146. I Want To Spread ................................................................. 232
147. A Fleeting Meteorite............................................................ 233
148. We Are Forever .................................................................... 234
149. A Yogi Tired Of Life ........................................................... 236
150. A Dream, Horrid and Surreal.............................................. 237
151. How Can I Conceal Myself? ................................................ 240
152. In Search Of A Question..................................................... 241
153. Where There Is Dark, There Is Light ................................. 242
154. I Am Smitten With You ...................................................... 243
155. Have You Ever Seen?........................................................... 244
156. An Eternal Enigma .............................................................. 245
157. I Preach Revolution ............................................................ 246
158. Path To The Unknown ....................................................... 249
159. How Dare You Trample?...................................................... 250
160. Every Moment Is A Challenge.............................................251
161. Illusion.................................................................................252
162. Journey Of My Life..............................................................253
163. Nature's Congruence............................................................ 254
164. Life Is An Enigma................................................................255
165. Look At Yourself ................................................................. 256
166. Inexplicable Enigma ............................................................ 257
167. I Feel Like Drinking The Moon.......................................... 258
168. And Time Prostrates ...........................................................259
169. The World Itself Has Turned Erotic ................................... 260
170. I Had Died A Thousand Times............................................ 261
171. How Astonishing! ............................................................... 262
172. Thus Reveal Themselves ..................................................... 263

173. America, You Must Be Stunned ..................... 264

174. You Are The One To Define The Order .................. 265

175. Profound Faith In Myself ............................... 266

176. I Have No Qualms...................................... 267

177. I Don't Know ......................................... 268

178. Naught Be Thy Destiny ................................ 269

179. Try Not To Incarcerate................................ 270

180. Morphed Into A Nymph ............................... 271

181. I Want To Spend ..................................... 272

182. How Long? .......................................... 273

183. Cadaverous Face.....................................274

184. While Reading Books ................................. 275

185. An Elusive Destination................................ 276

186. He Was Nowhere .................................... 277

187. Macbeths Of The World, Beware!...................... 278

188. But His Playthings ................................... 279

189. A Truth, Pure And Unvarnished ...................... 280

190. We Don't Believe..................................... 281

191. Time Would Have Mourned ........................... 282

192. Why Did You Make Us? .............................. 283

193. We Fear Everything Relating To Death.................. 284

194. Who Is Not Afraid Of It? ............................. 285

195. Time's Insanity...................................... 286

196. Every Week I Go To The Laundry...................... 287

197. Monarchy's Agony.................................... 288

198. I Don't Mind ........................................ 289

199. In My Dream ........................................ 290

200. I Cannot Remain Content ............................291

201. Romeo And Juliet .................................... 292

202. I Like Black The Most ................................ 293

203. A Mesmerizing Feat .................................. 294

204. A Sensual Pang....................................... 295

205. I Have Never Seen Myself ............................. 296

206. Poems Are Spontaneous Outbursts..................... 297

207. Conquering The Cosmos .............................. 298

208. Left In The Lurch .................................... 299

209. Insomniac Eyes ............................................................... 300

210. None To Console ............................................................. 301

211. O Loneliness! ................................................................. 302

212. O Paragon Of Beauty!...................................................... 303

213. House For Rent................................................................ 304

214. Spirit Of Sincere Empathy................................................ 305

215. History Is Replete ........................................................... 306

216. An Ode To Time ............................................................. 307

217. Fleeting Illusion ............................................................. 309

218. Human Blood ................................................................310

219. Ignore Me ....................................................................311

220. What Is Life If Not … .....................................................312

221. I Loved Everyone ...........................................................313

222. I Find You Everywhere ....................................................315

223. Thirst For Love ..............................................................316

224. Life Is Mesmerizing.........................................................317

225. Some Haikus..................................................................318

NOTES .....................................................................................335

# DEDICATION

Dedicated again to the great country, America,
the only *de facto* Hindu State on earth.

# MEA CULPA

This book is the continuation of the same vision, message, and mission my previous book, **America Tattwamasi**, published in 2016 had tried to convey. Named after the title poem 'America Arise And Awake', this book is a collection of poems that dive deep into human beings' atavistically intrinsic experience such as, pleasure and pain, agony and ecstasy, and life and death. Most of the poems, in a subtle way, strive to catapult readers into an ethereal realm where they come close to realizing their own Being.

As for the title poem, America Arise And Awake, it is a fervent attempt at reinvigorating this great country, America, that, above everything else, represents the supreme philosophy of freedom and liberty. The central message of this poem is that America's weakness and complacency will inexorably translate into the domination of entire world by authoritarian powers, predisposed to treating freedom and liberty as an anathema in the way of achieving their macabre goals. It is just because of this country's unswerving commitment to freedom and liberty that humanity has been able to see light at the end of the tunnel, authoritarian forces' consistent attempts at trampling on the conscience of human beings, notwithstanding. This poem further doubles down on this vision, and strongly advocates that America remain avidly proactive and assertive when it comes to promoting these values in different parts of the world.

Interestingly, referencing to the most defining moment of the *Mahabharata*, when Lord Krishna had revealed His true Being as the 'world-destroying Time' - this poem has passionately waxed wistful and prayed to America: "Just like all the mighty forces on earth hurriedly making their way into the cosmic mouth of the *Vishwaroop*, the mighty world-destroying Time, I want Russia, China, Iraq, Iran, North Korea, Yemen, Sudan, Egypt, Algeria, Libya, Syria, Venezuela, Cuba and the likes hurtle into your ever resplendent being, dazzling with the divine beauty and puissance of democracy, freedom and liberty". Meantime, in the comprehensive interest of freedom and liberty, a fitting blow delivered to rogue and callous authoritarianism, could also be the addition of a new dimension to American literature.

Equally worth mentioning is the fact that this poem has not shied away from touching upon the issues that have of late served to create unwanted divisions and cleavages in American society. With each side of the political divide trying to exploit every issue to its own advantage, without regard for fundamental values and institutions, the US Constitution and the Declaration of Independence have been meticulously nurturing for more than two centuries, politics seems to be reduced to mere zero sum game, something totally uncharacteristic of American democratic tradition. I don't think that it sounds cynical when I blame it on devious machinations, probably at the most subtlest possible level, on the part of inimical forces both within and without. Certainly there is not any dearth of forces that conspire to wrest control from us the leadership of contemporary world order, based on liberal democracy and capitalist free market economy. Series of incidents ranging from the desecration of our flag to the concoction of most sinister episodes, surrounding the highest institutions of this country, sounds to me the ominous vibrations of our enemies' portentous maneuverings, aimed at ultimately reducing us to a pipsqueak. Therefore, it is high time that we realized the truth and united under the respected Star Spangled Banner.

While depicting the brutal realities that have underscored our contemporary national politics, I might seem somewhat bitter and acerbic. However, I don't mean to be offensive towards any political forces. Neither do I want to disparage their conviction and commitment. What I am essentially concerned about is both the present and future of America and its great people whose empathy towards entire mankind has always remained nonpareil. Were it not for this country's abiding commitment to peace, prosperity, freedom and liberty for whole humankind, the face of this earth would certainly have been quite different - something akin to medieval nightmares. Amidst growing threat to international peace, prosperity, security and stability, especially on the part of revanchist, rogue and brutal authoritarian forces, holding the flag of freedom and liberty aloft is not that easy. However spasmodic, ominous rise of callous and ruthless terrorist organizations over the last many years, has also served to further complicate the situation. For an America divided unto itself, it is not that possible to cope with all these challenges. Neither can this country simply shrug off its responsibilities, bequeathed from its unswerving commitment to certain principles and ideals that have not only defined contemporary world order, but also contributed substantially to the advancement of human civilization.

Most of the poems in this book, in one way or another, echo the pristine message of the Upanishads, that are believed to have enunciated for the first time in recorded history of human beings the sacred mantra of freedom and liberty, by placing humans at the same pedestal as the Supreme entity, responsible for the creation and destruction of cosmos. Grand pronouncement of *'Aham Brahmashmi'* was not only an elemental challenge to condescending Creator, but also the revelation of immeasurable cosmic power, inherent in every human being. The same statement, by implicitly alluding to basic attributes of *Brahma*, has described each individual as a free spirit and an immortal Soul. In this context, I would like to reiterate my firm conviction that the basic ethos - marked by exceptional emphasis on individual freedom and liberty, and inherent trust in the impersonal Almighty - of the Constitution of the United States and the US Declaration of Independence, seems to be rooted in the Upanishadic doctrine of 'universality of spirit', whence spring basic attributes of America as a nation such as, democracy, human rights, rule of law, justice, equality and freedom. It is this conviction that prompted me to solemnly propose through **America Tattwamasi** that America be formally declared a Hindu State.

This book also represents a testament to my obsession with religion - the religion that is not inconsistent with the basic truth of science, the religion that encourages science to inquire into the nature of reality, and the religion that facilitates the internalization of 'unity of Soul', by seeking common grounds among ourselves, irrespective of color, creed, race, religion, ethnicity and origin. Meantime, the vehemence with which it has attacked so-called rites, rituals, customs and ceremonies - that, in collusion with corrupt and kleptomaniac priesthood, serve to decimate religions - is most likely to resonate with the intrinsic ethos of contemporary world, betrothed as it is to reason and rationality. Besides, special emphasis has been laid on the creation of a new religious order that will recognize Krishna, Jesus and Muhammad not as an end, but only as means, through which each individual on earth can realize that he is God unto himself.

While writing these lines, I am not singing the praise of my poems. Neither am I disposed to self-aggrandizement. I am just making a sincere effort to clarify myself with regard to certain issues that tend to strike chord with today's human society. Even if it is considered contrary to customary practice and tradition for the author himself to comment on his writing, I would humbly request enlightened readers to acknowledge it as my pleading of mea culpa.

Ramesh Sharma
Massachusetts, USA

# AMERICA ARISE AND AWAKE!

The soil of this country carries the fecundity of human endeavor.
The air of this country spews the fragrance of human ingenuity.
The space of this country echoes the music of human excellence.
The water of this country reveals the solemn undulation of human imagination.
The light of this country radiates the depth of human conscience.
The ambience of this country defines the spirituality of human existence.

America,
In your equanimity is reflected human beings' tryst with divinity.
And in your steadfastness, heavenly beauty of harmony with Nature.
When you sit in meditation, the world finds its *kundalini* awakened.
When you suffer the pangs of conscience, the world gets sucked into the vortex of chaos and confusion.

You are the purity of Jesus' love;
Krishna's philosophy of karma you are.
You are the solemn compassion of the Buddha;
Glorious valor of Mohammad you are.

America, I adore your divine Self that illuminates the three worlds – physical, astral and causal.
I offer my obeisance and prayers unto the God that you are.
You shine like the most effulgent sun in the destiny of mankind.
May you enlighten our intellect and purify our Soul.

America, you are the one through which mysteries of the universe can be uncovered.
You are the one that propels Nature to unfold itself without its divine beauty and celestial luster being obscured.

You are the one that persuades the Almighty to commiserate with humans on no less a footing than that of Himself.

You are the one that divines the full potential of infinity in each individual.

You are the one that makes each individual aware of his own purity and perfection.

You are the one that can render the bond among humans melodious and enriching.

You are the one through which humanity can embark on a sacred mission of purity and strength.

You are the one whose extraordinary vision has enlightened humans about the nature of reality.

You are the one on whom is pinned the advancement of human civilization, with all its sacredness intact.

You are the one who wields the power of catapulting humans into the realm of transport by making them realize their true Being.

America, since you are the epitome of freedom and liberty - the ultimate destination of entire creation - you are divine unto yourself.

America, I implore you to reinvigorate yourself as a force, determined to inspire human beings across the globe to revolt against tyranny and injustice.

Why should one and a half billion Chinese be stripped of their inalienable right to freedom and liberty?

Why should they be subjugated under the tyrannical regime of a bunch of thugs who thrive in the decimation of peoples' conscience?

Why should they be subjected to perennial intimidation and frowning of a group of unscrupulous ideologues?

Why should they be made hostage to diabolic ambitions of ruthless party stalwarts?

Why should they keep kowtowing to whimsical diktats of unprincipled kleptomaniacs?

Why should they be robbed of their rights to democracy, human rights and rule of law?

Why are the Chinese made to feel that they are nothing but robotic androids, created by the helmsmen, just to serve as lubricant of the gigantic communist machine?

Why is the conscience of one fifth of world population splashed with the putrescent interpretation of human dignity and honor?

Why should the international community bear the brunt of a wayward giant's devious recourse to brazen defiance and recalcitrance?

Why should small neighbors find themselves intimidated and threatened by soaring territorial ambitions of the communist juggernaut?

Why should fundamentals of global order, based on liberal democracy and free market capitalist economy, be twisted to suit the illegitimate interests of amoral apparatchiks?

Why should we continue to sheepishly countenance massive theft and espionage they have been carrying out for years?

Why should we sacrifice our innovation and inventions at the altar of their bizarre stealth?

How can world community remain mere a passive spectator to the domineering dragon's steady slide towards yet another bout of orthodox Maoist tyranny?

I am a poet of boldness, courage and bravery.

I hate pusillanimity and cowardice.

I abominate obsequiousness, submission and quiescence.

I am foreign to the sophistry of mincing words.

I have a trenchant abhorrence for cowardice when it comes to safeguarding freedom and liberty.

I want to see fiery lava flow in the veins of youths, not chilled water.

I want them to rise in revolt against any force - no matter how colossal - that tramples on their freedom and liberty.

Even the worth of life - if subdued and humiliated - cannot outweigh the grandeur and majesty of freedom.

Freedom is the most precious crown of human conscience, liberty the authentic definition of our existence.

Devoid of these jewels, dignity and honor of humanity suffer ignominious atrophy.

Why can't 23 million people of Taiwan enjoy their inalienable rights to freedom and liberty?
Why should they find themselves mired in sordid morass, under the gigantic feet of a primeval dragon?
What is preventing them from entering the celestial realm of independence?
No less agonizing is the plight of Tibetans who seem to have been betrayed by none other than their own temporal/spiritual leader.
Virtually left in the lurch, they think they have no choice but to immolate themselves.
To me, it sounds utterly unconscionable.
Self-immolation does not lead to freedom and liberty.
Rather it leads to sacrilege and desecration of the Self within you.

I am an active volcano.
I have insatiable fire within me.
The liquid inferno swirling in my conscience is impatient to embrace humanity, with the pious message of revolution.
Revolt, revolt, and revolt!
*Klaibyam masmagama …*
*Uttishthata, jagrata …*
No supernatural force is going to bestow you with the divine blessing of freedom and liberty.
You and you yourself must strive for it.
Knock and certainly it will be opened unto you.
O my hapless fellow humans of China, Taiwan and Tibet,
arise and awake!
Don't make a delay in raising the flag of freedom and liberty.
I love you; I have enormous empathy towards you.
I know you are none other than myself.
I get traumatized when the heavy boots of doctrinaire thugs trample on your head.
I start writhing in agony when the dehumanizing machine of their military industrial complex tries to pulverize your conscience.
The most egregious mortal injury the Tiananmen had inflicted on your psyche is still continuing to torture me.

How can I forget the demonic ruthlessness meted out to the innocent mass that had expressed its pent up craving for democracy and self-determination?

I possess a unique constitution.
I cannot remain quiescent until each individual on earth is guaranteed his inalienable divine rights to freedom and liberty.
I see for myself liberation, deliverance, moksha, and nirvana in my undying concern for fellow humans.
Nothing on earth can constrain me within the artificial boundaries, carved out by mortal entities.
My dear fellow beings, you are my religion, you are my spirituality, you are my faith, and you are my God.
You are my journey, and you are my destination.
No doubt, I am a Hindu.
I see millions of Gods and deities in your pious existence.
I can realize the Absolute by meditating on you.
You are both my *atma* and *paramatma*.
In you and only you, I get my *atma* integrated with the *paramatma*.
I am a pilgrim, and you my holy pilgrimage.
You are my temple, church, mosque and monastery.
I disdain being chained by archaic rites, rituals, ceremonies and tradition.
But I esteem their innate significance - if there is any - in which is shrouded the absolute nature of reality.
I am free; I always cherish freedom.
Not only for myself, but for whole mankind.
I don't want to be embroiled in nebulous discourses of religion and philosophy.
I don't want to be lost in the dark alley of their redundant rigmarole.
I hate reveling in their nauseating mumbo jumbo.
I don't want them to contort my vision of humanity.
Religion sans humanity is a curse, and philosophy sans humanity an anathema.
O my fellow beings, arise above this curse and anathema.
You are yourself the sum and substance of religion.
You are yourself the core of philosophy.

O priests, pastors, pandas, mullahs and monks, just let your respective
Gods and Goddesses free.
Don't ever try to enchain them with your moronic interpretations of
scriptures.
Don't ever try to incarcerate them in the penitentiary of your lust,
ignorance and superstition.
Just let them free.
Let them be one with humans, just like Krishna and gopikas.

O impostors of the spiritual world, you might be surprised to hear me.
You might be livid at my 'audacity and effrontery'.
Listen, your blasphemy is religion to me, and your apostasy spirituality.
I don't care even if the entire monuments of bricks and mortars are
demolished as long as we see God in human Soul.
You have turned those monuments into prisons where Krishna, Jesus,
Mohammad and the Buddha have been incarcerated.
Amidst high volume music, you pretend to pray, so people outside
cannot hear their cry for humanity.
As if serving as a mediator, you conspire to widen the gap between
humans and them.
Prodded by greed and desire, you try to drive a wedge between God and
humans.

You imbecile nincompoops!
Those whom you have incarcerated in those monuments are not real
Gods, rather they are only the effigies.
Even if you burn them, it does not make any difference.
Immortal and eternal, Gods have already shifted to the Soul of human
beings.
Burn entire Holy scriptures.
Humanity will be illuminated.
Destroy entire Holy monuments.
Humans will be rejuvenated.
Demolish entire faiths.
Divinity will reveal itself.

Even the death of cosmos cannot destroy Gods that reside in human Soul.

And this is what defines the endless saga of creation, sustenance and destruction.

*Ayam atma brahma* – It is human Soul whence springs the cosmos, with its endless cycles of birth and death.

Hidden behind the cosmic paraphernalia - such as, black holes, wormholes, quasars, galaxies, stars, planets, nebulae, dark energy, dark matter, et al, - is the human Soul, the sole cause of these eternal phenomena.

O human, the cosmos along with its infinitively expansive family, revolves around your Soul.

It does not have any cause save divinity, radiating from your Soul, to predicate its birth and existence on.

O human, how fortunate you are!

How glorious you are!

My deepest obeisance unto the truth, hidden behind your transcendental existence.


O ninnies of the spiritual world!

Come out of the tiny water pool, and try to expand your vision across the vast and fathomless oceans.

Don't ever try to confine Gods to tiny bodies of some prophets and messengers.

He is way above them, too.

Way above your clouded vision and circumscribed imagination.

O villains of the spiritual world!

Since thousands of years, you have been trying to exact ransoms by abducting Gods and deities.

You have been trying to blackmail innocent devotees.

You have been purveying superstition, bigotry and fanaticism.

You have been trying to hoodwink us into believing that Gods are synonymous with the inanimate structures of bricks and mortars.

You have been trying to bamboozle us into believing that Gods cannot transcend the barriers of your making.

You want us to believe that you are the ones who can twist Gods around your fingers.

You have been trying to befool us into believing that Gods can be easily bribed.

You have been trying to make us believe that Gods are inherently inclined to harbor discrimination on the basis of race, religion, caste, creed, ethnicity and origin.

Worse still, you want us to believe that Gods sanction atrocities against one's adversaries.

You are even trying to brainwash us into believing that we should embark on unspeakable pogrom and holocaust, when it comes to fulfilling our ambitions, no matter how diabolic.

You want us to sing praise of your crimes against humanity and human beings.

O abominable desperadoes of the spiritual world!

Unlike some fairy tales, the Soul of Gods does not reside in the dark, dingy and dank confinements of bricks and mortars; rather it dwells in the ever-effulgent, effervescent, and immortal Soul of humans.

Archaic treatises and inanimate monuments can never outweigh the worth of human beings who are Gods unto themselves.

This is God's injunction.

Even God cannot see anything but Himself in his creation.

He will find His own existence drab and vacuous without the appreciation of humans.

He will be reduced to a wizened flower, devoid of its fragrance.

Gods are the shadows of human beings, not the other way around.

It might sound blasphemous to you.

I don't care; I don't agree with your definition of God.

To me, humans are the most vivid definition of God.

God with whom I am so obsessed is not a deadwood.

He is the infinite power that can easily devour the cosmos.

He is the eternal power that even the cosmos' endless cycles of birth and death cannot outlive.

He is the unimaginable fire that can engulf and instantly reduce the whole cosmos to ashes.

My fellow beings, you might be surprised to hear my words.

These are not my words; I am just echoing the voice of God within yourself.

I can see the same power hidden in your Soul.

Come on! Let's realize it.

You can realize it in the revolution against tyranny and injustice.

You can realize it in the rebellion against thuggery and ruthlessness of brutal regimes.

You can realize it in the resistance against suppression and savagery of demonic forces.

You can realize it in the crusade against satanic powers.

You can realize it in the jihad against dehumanizing authoritarianism and cruel dictatorships.

You can realize it in the annihilation of heinous forces, bent on destroying humans and humanity.

My dear fellow beings of the world, come on!

Let's hearken to the message of immortality, seers and sages of the Upanishads had spoken thousands of years ago.

They are true when they say that we are the 'children of immortal bliss'.

Nothing can enervate us; nothing can destroy us.

Come on, let's arise and awake!


O my fellow beings of North Korea, I have enormous love for you.

I want you all to respond to the call of your own conscience.

Freedom and liberty are your inalienable fundamental rights.

You have every right to defenestrate the brutal regime that is hell bent on crushing your conscience.

No power on earth has the right to constrain you from defying the ruthless tyranny.

I have unwavering confidence in the colossal power of your Soul.

Come on! Realize the insurmountable power, hidden within yourselves.

Throw that dark symbol of ignominy into the dustbin of history.

No force on earth can strip you of your rights to democracy, human rights and rule of law.

As the children of immortal bliss, you have every right to determine your own destiny.

Have courage and carve out the path of your liberation yourself.

Entire faiths and religions of the world have a message for you – arise and awake!

Do away with this heinous criminality, weighing mortally on the destiny of 25 million noble souls.

How long can you endure the perennial humiliation and unending censure of your own conscience?

How long can you tolerate being trampled under the sacrilegious boots of inhuman thugs?

How long can you condone the brutal pulverization of your own Being?

My dear brothers and sisters of North Korea, in the name of humanity, I call upon you all to listen to the voice of God within you who seems desperate to see you freed from this hellish nightmare.

May you all have enough courage as to listen to His voice within yourselves.

May your Gods bless you all.


O America, the paragon of freedom and liberty, how can you condone the devilish tyranny being meted out to millions upon millions of people on earth?

I wonder why you cannot give voice to their agony and torture under the leadership of an eccentric despot?

I wonder why you cannot help hapless North Koreans redeem themselves from the diabolic clutch of a demonic regime?

I wonder why you cannot safeguard the innocents from being executed at the hands of a callous dictator?

I wonder why you seem completely indifferent to their amassing of lethal weaponry, only to make freedom and liberty hostage to their nuclear and ballistic blackmail?

I wonder why your unswerving commitment to democracy and freedom tapers off when it comes to challenging that recalcitrant order?

I wonder why your adherence to humane values appears to shrink when exposed to the butchery of the North?

I wonder with still deep regret why your divine mantra 'We the People' finds itself subdued under the tyrannical cacophony of a devil?

America, O uncontested leader of the free world, how can it be possible for you to turn a deaf ear on the lament of Warmbier's Soul that has been incessantly echoing the agony and anguish of millions upon millions of people of that Stalinist gulag?

America, arise and awake!
It is incumbent upon you to deliver this world from ruthless tyranny and callous despotism.
It is incumbent upon you to adorn each and every individual on earth with the most precious crown of 'We the People'.
It is incumbent upon you to emancipate human race from dehumanizing repression and atrocities.
It is incumbent upon you to usher in a new era of hope and optimism in the otherwise despondent world.
It is incumbent upon you to make each and every individual realize the enormous divine potential, lurking behind his own Being.
It is incumbent upon you to make the world community realize the existence of heaven here on earth.
America, you must realize that the entire world is your sovereignty:
When it comes to bestowing mankind with freedom and liberty;
When it comes to making them realize the blessing of rule of law;
When it comes to making them exercise true democracy and human rights;
When it comes to making them realize the true essence of equality and justice.
America, how can you address intrinsic concerns of humanity unless you realize yourself the cosmic potential, hidden behind your own Being?
Therefore, America, I beseech you from the bottom of my heart.
America, the pious symbol of freedom and liberty,
America, the greatest philosophy of humanity,
America, the only savior of human race,
Arise and awake!

I am an untiring witness to human history.
Nothing pertaining to the journey of human beings can escape my prescient gaze.
I have seen them wander from place to place in search of food and shelter.

I have seen them traverse an unimaginably long distance in search of comfort and security.

I have seen them scale seemingly insurmountable mountains in search of height and loftiness.

I have seen them fathom the bottom of oceans in search of depth and profundity.

I have seen them appreciate creations of Nature in search of beauty and fragrance.

I have seen them adore the vastness of cosmos in search of magnanimity and munificence.

I have seen them explore the universe in search of expansive horizon of their vision.

I have seen them identify the last frontier of cosmos in search of their own Being.

I have seen them discover the truth, behind the relation between time and space, in search of their own existence.

Revealingly, I have seen them dive into nothingness in search of nothingness, underscoring the nothingness of their existence that consummates in nothing but nothingness.

I have seen them in turn come to the conclusion that life is a journey of nothingness, with nothing but nothingness as its destination.

*'Brahmaiva tena gantabyam …'*

What an auspicious pilgrimage!

And what a propitious journey!

Really, how enigmatic we are!

I do appreciate everything that gives meaning to the journey of human race.

I am here to boost humans and humanity.

As a poet of human beings and humanity, I have transcended all barriers that try to confine us to watertight compartments of race and religion, caste and color, ethnicity and origin, and geography and geopolitics.

I see them all as just humans, the bridge between the heaven and earth.

America, you are the one that always inspires me to seek my Self. Sometimes, it seems to me as if my journey is but a mirage, lost in eternal illusion.

At other times, I think life is something that always demands substance and profundity.

What is life if not a quest for substance and profundity?

Are we mere illusion?

Is this universe mere a reflection of our illusion?

Is our journey an abstract expression of our quest?

Not thousands, but millions of questions besiege me.

To me, each individual is a question in himself.

He himself is an answer, too.

One cannot answer the question of the other.

One has to answer himself.

Even the universe cannot be the answer to our questions.

Rather, it is an eternal provocation that always evokes our imagination and ingenuity.

Human life is a cosmic waltz that we dance together with heavenly bodies.

Although we get along with them, we tend to feel, we cannot morph ourselves into something celestial.

Perhaps the gravity of earth always pulls us down to the mundane world.

And we tend to define ourselves as mortals, prone to the cycle of life and death.

But we forget that even heavenly bodies are not immune to this cycle of absolute truth.


Truly speaking, I am wary of talking about politics that pushes us down the morass of profane expediency.

Neither do I want to utter even a single word that serves to lacerate the sensibilities of my own fellow Americans.

But when I find my country and its sacred values jeopardized by preposterous acts and pronouncements, my conscience forthwith exhorts me to speak the truth.

Then I start questioning myself:

Why are we trying to unleash lethal Electro Magnetic Impulse of opposition, aimed at delegitimizing the newly-elected President?

Why have we chosen to embark on preposterous propaganda, visibly with the sole object of tarnishing the highest office of the nation?

Why do we stoop so low as to insinuate the Commander-in-Chief's collusion with an arch enemy?

Why are we hell bent on forcing the Captain to yield to enemies' treacherous machinations?

Why are we taking sledgehammer to the basic foundation of our democratic system and tradition?

Why are we emboldening our adversaries by weakening the basic structure of our democracy?

Why are we trying to jeopardize peoples' confidence in democratic values and institutions?

Why are we trying to vitiate our glorious tradition of tolerance by smearing the newly elected leader of the country?

Why are we trying to undo the legitimacy of elections, without any substantial evidence?

My fellow Americans, I respect your disagreement and dissent.
I have high regard for your conviction and commitment.
I fully respect your rights to freedom of speech and peaceful assembly.
I do humbly beseech you to beware me if I ever breach the dignity and decorum while expressing my respectful disagreements with you.
I have absolutely no intention of impugning your patriotic fervor.
But when I find ourselves dishonor our own democratic rights, I feel very sorry.
When I find ourselves distort the reality and facts, only to serve some wayward impulse, I feel really sorry.
When I find ourselves overstep the parameter of dignity and honor, just to vent our pent-up angst and animosity, I feel really sorry.
When I find ourselves resort to vulgarity and bizarre expressions, that tend to tarnish reverential symbols and images of this country, I really feel very sorry.
When I find ourselves descend into ignominy and paranoia in the face of someone's rise, I feel really very sorry.
When I find ourselves negatively indifferent to the strengthening of democratic values and institutions, I feel really very sorry.
No less sorry am I at the sight of media relegate itself to a pernicious mouthpiece of vengeance and outrage.

I feel really very sorry when I find ourselves nurture our ambition at the cost of America and its innocent people.

I feel very sorry when I find ourselves collude, wittingly or unwittingly, with our arch-enemies for nothing but to advance our illegitimate claims.

I feel very sorry when I find ourselves trample on democratic norms and practices, just to stigmatize the image of political opponents.

I feel really very sorry when I find ourselves desperate to grab power even by means, foul and indignant.

I feel very sorry when I find ourselves smear the institution of Captaincy in order to justify our unjustifiable claims.

I really feel very sorry when I find ourselves embark on disinformation campaign, with complete disregard for objective facts.

I really feel very sorry when I find ourselves launch into preposterous harangues, solely aimed at the contortion of truth.

I feel very sorry when I find ourselves misconstrue the magnanimity of this country as to suit some awkward temperament.

I feel very sorry when I find ourselves misinterpret our sacred documents, presumably with a view to sating inherent prejudices.

I really feel very sorry when I find ourselves completely impervious to the heinous crimes, committed on our innocent compatriots by alien desperadoes.

I feel really very sorry when I find ourselves scandalously indifferent to the worsening law and order situation on account of barbaric pyromaniacs.

I really feel very sorry when I find our conscience darkened by vindictive impulse.

I really feel extremely sorry when I find our judgment clouded by base emotions.

My fellow Americans, I don't have any animosity against you.
I love you as much as I love myself.
We all share same values and institutions that have long been fostered and nurtured by the Constitution and the US Declaration of Independence.
We are all guided by the lofty principles, based on 'universality of spirit'.

As Americans, we breathe love; we live love.

Love is our principle, and love our ideal.

Inspired by this philosophy, we trust in God, inherent in each human being.

But, my fellow Americans, don't make a mistake:

Love for us is not a mawkish outburst of the meek.

It is not a plaintive cry of a lachrymose heart.

Rather, love for us is the chivalry of the knight.

Knighthood bathed in sublime compassion.

We love entire mankind on earth.

We do extend our magnanimity towards all – dispossessed, repressed, marginalized, oppressed, tortured and persecuted.

But that does not mean that:

We should allow our love to be a recipe for the destruction of our own country and its people;

We should allow our magnanimity to be the cause of our own devastation;

We should not close our borders even to those who are inimical to our values;

We should be liberal even to those who are hell bent on destroying our freedom and liberty;

We should be courteous to those whose sole mission of life is to destabilize our country;

We should be kind to those who are determined to eliminate our existence;

We should share our country even with those who want to exterminate us en masse.


Was coexistence possible between Jesus and the Scribes and Pharisees who were determined to eliminate the former?

What was it that ignited the great war between the Pandavas and Kauravas at Kurukshetra?

Why coexistence was not possible between those two clans, even though they both shared the same ancestry?

Why was coexistence not possible between the Axis and the Allied powers?

Why did the human race plunge into such a devastating war that killed 60 million people?

These are some of the hard-boiled questions that always try to mock mankind.

To me the answer is simple: it was inevitable.

Isn't is utter naiveté to conjure up an idyllic coexistence between the good and evil?

What good are faith and religion if they inspire us to submit ourselves sheepishly to the pogrom of evil that is inveterately committed to the destruction of truth, justice and righteousness?

What good is love if it handsomely rewards cruelty, untruth and injustice, instead of upholding civilizational values, such as peace, harmony and coexistence?

In its long history of existence, human race has many a time found itself at the crossroads of existential dilemmas.

And not humans, but their fate has always preempted with its own decision, however macabre and apocalyptic.

And we, as humans, have always consciously countenanced the diktat of fate, no matter how painful and torturous.

To some, it might simply be a plaything at the hands of divine providence.

It could also be the routine reordering of divine scheme of things.

It is politics that has always determined the course of history.

Religion and faith have proved to be its rather uneasy bedfellows.

Politics can neither spurn, nor does it have the capability to fully embrace them.

My dear fellow Americans, I have my own take on politics and governance.

Politics is not a utopian realm of mere ideal and wishful thinking.

In politics, a rose is rose; not a tender heart of one's beloved.

Politics does not know the language of poetry.

Politics is invariably related to theatrics and gesticulations.

The world of politics is always found to be infested by devious vermin that thrive in inherent human vulnerabilities.

Politics has always been used as an art of converting peoples' aspirations and shortcomings into something that enables its actors to have control over their fate.

Politics does not respect religion, neither does it honor spirituality and faith.

Rather it exploits them, only to enhance its macabre piquancy.

The pedigree of politics has always remained the same; only its histrionics have changed.

The struggle between its adamance and our reluctance to submit tends to underscore the development of human civilization.

It is an earnest yearning on the part of people around the world that politicians be sincere and committed to the cause of humans and humanity.

But good politicians are at most a balanced and judicious combination of Machiavelli and Gandhi.

The rest represent the echo of devils and monsters that have often served to influence the march of human civilization.

Isn't it a stunning irony?

Leaders like Lincoln and Mandela are but precious exceptions.


America, arise and awake!

Don't let yourself be an object of travesty and mockery.

You have enormous power to lead the world.

Your abiding commitment to freedom and liberty morally authorizes you to shepherd whole mankind.

Entire globe is your sovereignty, provided you commit yourself to the prosperity and happiness of mankind leaving on earth.

You have earned this position not by saber-rattling, but by sharing your affection with all people of this world.

Look at the global vibration that each and every action on your part tends to create.

Were it not for the thirst for your embrace, why would even the people of your adversaries get paranoid at the temporary decrees, asking them not to enter this land?

Were it not for the fervent penchant for being dissolved into your being, why would the world populace descend into hysteria in response to your temporary restrictions on refugees?

America, global attraction towards you has certainly added to your responsibility.

You cannot simply shrug it off.

Riding on the wave of this soaring fascination, America, you should set yourself on the path of destroying evils, intent on jeopardizing peace and harmony, cooperation and coexistence.

Humanity is impatient to witness the obsequies of tyranny, despotism, and dictatorship at the mighty hands of freedom and liberty, enshrined in your Constitution and the Declaration of Independence.

No powers – both within and without – should be allowed to stymie your march towards this august mission.

Past is reminiscence, and future hallucination.

America, now is the right moment to put each and every evil on earth to death.

The evil of untruth, the evil of injustice, the evil of inequality, the evil of atrocity, the evil of subjugation,

The evil of intimidation, the evil of coercion, the evil of terrorism, the evil of extremism, the evil of conspiracy and murder.

The evil of starvation, the evil of discrimination, the evil of nepotism, the evil of cronyism, the evil of despotism, the evil of autocracy, the evil of corruption, the evil of disempowerment, the evil of nuclear and ballistic blackmail, the evil of fanaticism and bigotry.

Let evils around the world realize that their days are but numbered.

O lord of truth and justice, have mercy upon human race.

Now is the time to raise your divine scepter.

Death shall be your option.

Death shall be your weapon.

Death shall be your mission.

I am so passionately talking about death, because I preach death.

Come on, my fellow beings of this planet, hearken to my sermon on death!

I preach death.

The death that is more precious than life.

The death without which life cannot exist.

The death that adds luster to life.

The death that transcends entire inhibitions of existence.

The death that morphs humans into Gods.

The death that helps you identify yourself with your Being.

The death that inspires you to explore your latent potential.

The death that leads to immortality.

The death that gives purpose and meaning to your life.

The death that makes you the Supreme.

The death that does not cherish blood, but promotes love and compassion.

The death that does not unleash chaos and confusion, but nurtures peace and harmony.

The death that does not kill, but gives life to the weak and meek.

The death that reminds one of the sacrifice of Jesus.

The death that rejuvenates the Buddha in each individual.

The death that resurrects Krishna's philosophy of karma in the heart of human race.

And finally the death that leads us from untruth to truth, from darkness to light and from mortality to immortality.

Death is the cathartic denouement of a long discourse on success and failure, ecstasy and agony, and victory and defeat.

O children of immortality!

You are not mere a clot of blood.

Henceforward you will realize your true nature.

You are immune to all kinds of afflictions.

You are even above your own mind, body, sense and intellect.

You are the master of your Self.

Let me illumine you with this divine revelation.

Come on, have courage to accept my precious offer.

Upon whom shall I bestow this divine gift, save you?

I love you, I empathize you, I cherish you.

Let me stroke your bedraggled hair with utmost affection.

Let me caress you with divine sublimity.

Let me infuse divine solemnity into your broken heart.

Let me anoint your lacerated existence with the blessing of love.

Let me dissolve myself into your being to emerge one with the Absolute.

I am an innovator par excellence.

Let me innovate a new tradition of defiance, rebellion and revolt.

Scholars, researchers, writers and litterateurs of the world, do not expect me to honor the past.

I am not here to uphold any tradition of the past, or for that matter, established norms and practices.

Rather I am determined to dismantle them.

Since they have failed to keep pace with the time and space, they have lost their relevance.

To me they have already become hackneyed and stereotyped.

I call for a new dynamism that dovetails rapidly developing human consciousness.

How can I uphold them when they have become so anachronistic and obsolete?

Don't expect me to uphold even the rules of your so-called grammar and literature, much less the codes of life.

I will create my own grammar.

I will create my own language.

I will create my own literature.

I want to be the author of a new grammar, language and literature of life.

I am no more interested in writing letters, words and sentences.

I am inclined to write blood, heart and spirit.

I want to write humans with the ink of humanity.

I want to create a collage of human attributes, brimming with divine spirit.

Maybe, my writing does not fit in with your definition of poetry.

Why do I need to care about your definition?

I don't care about that.

Neither your blandishment nor your intimidation can persuade me to toe your definition.

I am absolutely free from all kinds of chains of yours.

Neither your parameter can discipline me, nor can your limitations constrain my thinking.

I write what I think is right, no matter how absurd and horrific it might sound to your circumscribed consciousness.

There is a great difference between you and me.

Unlike you, I have seen innumerable civilizations of the past.

You have rendered yourself evanescent by being confined to a few.

You have been dwarfed by your own myopic vision.

Your definition of literature is determined by scores of artificial forces, ensuing from human passions, prejudices and impulses, combined with reflexive societal reactions.

A vast cosmos, unfolding itself in its dazzling splendor, bedecks my definition of literature.

You might see humans from three or four dimensions in extremis.

I can see them from millions of dimensions.

You can see nothing more than a puny human being in humans.

I can see the entire cosmos in them.

You try to define humans in terms of biology, chemistry and physics.

I define them in terms of sacred Soul.

Your approach to humans is at best based on humanity, whereas mine is based on divinity.

A human to you is an end in himself.

But to me, he is part of the continuum.

You look at the beauty of his body.

I peer into his Being.

I am always focused on subjects whereas you are fixated on their elusive reflections.

You tend to measure humans in terms of pounds and kilograms.

I measure them in terms of divine potential.

You cannot challenge even mundane institutions.

I dare transcend the authority of Gods.

You cower at the sight by life.

Even death gets scared of me.

Therefore, O researchers, scholars, writers and litterateurs of the world, don't seek scholarship and erudition in my writing.

I never write to be a scholar or an erudite intellectual.

I never give a damn to your applause, no matter how magniloquent.

I am proud to be myself.

Unlike you, I don't need to be accountable to anyone, save my own Soul.

I am Time.

O America, arise and awake!

Listen to the voice of my Soul.

You are the supreme empire ever created on earth.

All people on earth seem desperate to come under your sovereignty.
They are impatient to obey your injunctions and commandments.
You represent the greatest sermon based on the universality of Soul.
Under your aegis, tortured mankind expects to find solace of the
Himalayan solitude.
O America, stand up to their expectations, and fulfill their desire.
Make yourself robust and resilient, so the pace of time can adjust itself
to your clairvoyant personality.
Shake off obsolete antiquities that seem tempted to tarnish your image,
as the divine embodiment of freedom and liberty.
Don't let any force trample on your pious mission – the mission to
bestow the blessing of freedom and liberty on beleaguered human race.
Just like an innocent child, sometimes I feel like I am inclined to
question your adherence to some seemingly moronic principles.
How come the justices of the Court are privileged to exercise near divine
authority?
If they are really supreme as to adjudicate the destiny of our
Constitution and this great nation, why are they defined in terms of
party lines?
Why do they tend to wallow in partisan politics to the detriment of
comprehensive national interests?
How come they have been provided with a pedestal that even the
representatives of people cannot match?
Even having been bestowed with such unparalleled power, authority
and respect, how come they can identify themselves with some partisan
proclivities and prejudices?
I know, the provision of check and balance is one of the most beautiful
ornaments of our Constitution.
But I always wonder if those, who place their personal predisposition
ahead of America and the American people, can earnestly appreciate this
beauty.
I really don't think the emperor is naked.
But certainly there are forces that tend to relish voyeurism.

America, I chastise you, I criticize you, I admonish you, I challenge you,
I fault you, but not out of hatred against your persona.

I embark on such impulses out of deep and abiding commitment to you, as an eternal embodiment of democracy, freedom and liberty.

I want to see in you the mightiest empire ever created by human civilizations.

The empire of love and affection, the empire of magnanimity and munificence, the empire of empathy and compassion, the empire of altruism and selflessness.

And certainly the empire of extraordinary power and prowess that no evil force can even dare challenge.

Just like all the mighty forces on earth hurriedly making their way into the cosmic mouth of the *Vishwaroop*, the mighty world-destroying Time, I want Russia, China, Iraq, Iran, North Korea, Yemen, Sudan, Egypt, Algeria, Libya, Venezuela, Cuba and the likes hurtle into your ever resplendent Being, dazzling with the divine beauty and puissance of democracy, freedom and liberty.

I want every individual on earth to enjoy the life of full dignity and honor, under the sovereign wing of your loftiness.

There will be no religions prejudiced against human beings and humanity.

There will be no faiths harboring discrimination among the children of immortality.

There will be no conviction inconsistent with the oneness of human race.

There will be no belief system thriving in the blood of the innocents.

There will be no dogma nurtured by the lethal blend of misogynistic outlook and xenophobic fervor.

Entire world will be illumined by your impassioned advocacy of universality of spirit.

America, you will be the true messenger of spiritual wisdom, bequeathed from great seers and sages of the Upanishads, the light of human consciousness.

Mother of all religions, the Upanishads are the ultimate truth wherefrom springs our knowledge of science and spirituality.

Ten times ten is equal to one hundred.

Ten subtracted from ten is equal to zero.

Ten plus ten is equal to twenty.

Ten divided by ten is equal to one.

No doubt, this is mathematics.

To me, this is not only mathematics but also the fundamental message of the Upanishads.

Upanishads are not vapid outbursts of emotion.

They are both journey and destination of science.

They provide spiritual veneer to science.

It was the Upanishads that for the first time in human history fathomed the mystery of the universe, by revealing the existence of indestructible power, enveloping the cosmos.

Meantime, they have posed a momentous challenge to modern science by identifying human beings with that imperishable and omnipotent power.

Not least, by expounding the extraordinary doctrine of universality of spirit, the Upanishads have provided a clear direction to all disciplines of human creativity and imagination.

They are in themselves a caveat too: 'See oneself in all, or perish en masse'.


I see this world, along with the immense cosmos, bustling with innumerable heavenly bodies.

But do I really see it, or someone within me makes me feel as if I myself am seeing this all?

Do my eyes really see them?

Who is this I who claims to have seen all those entities?

Is it my ego or my servitude to some unseen force?

How can I identify this I who claims to have provided me with the panoramic view of this cosmos?

Is it someone who creates, sustains and dissolves the cosmos?

Is it someone who tries to have control over me through the multitude of natural forces?

Or is it someone who pretends to be my Self and makes me dance to his tune?

Are these really so-called modes of *prakriti* that try to enslave me, by enticing away from my own Self?

And what is this all drama staged by different *gunas* – *satwa*, *rajas* and *tamas*?

Who is the real kingpin behind all these dramatis personae, involving mind, intellect, ego, *prakriti* and *gunas*?

Are these mere illusion, aimed at getting me enmeshed in esoteric complexities and byzantine enigmas?

Where does the definition of God fit into this sprawling mystery?

How does all this relate me to the unimaginable machinations and shenanigans of celestial entities, while spawning series of realignments to suit their vested interests?

Am I, supposedly the true manifestation of the Supreme Being, responsible for the violence, perpetrated in a cosmic scale by the constant collisions between heavenly rivals?

America, I am tying to seek answers to myriads of questions in your existence, as a paragon of freedom and liberty.

To me you represent the sacred symbol '*Om*'.

You represent something extremely subtle, and beyond the comprehension of lowbrow mind.

Even the dissolution of this universe cannot render you extinct.

Because the cosmos might disappear but the transcendental urge for freedom will never die.

It was the transcendental urge for freedom that brought this universe into existence.

It might again be the same urge that will bring this universe to an end, most presumably to achieve still higher goal.

This cycle will thus go on and on, without any interruption.

This is what has been happening eternally.

Both the beginning and end of the cosmos can be attributed to mythical Brahma's characteristic penchant for absolute freedom.

Freedom is the transcendental rendezvous where both beginning and the end meet in a spirit of kindred unity.

America, you are the bridge between these two ends.

You are the iridescent spectrum that constantly radiates the colorful visage of transcendental unity between the beginning and the end.

You are the most beautiful melody, flowing from the celestial union between two ends of the spectrum.

In your spirit is eternally embedded the insatiate urge for freedom and liberty.

It has inexorably morphed you into something immortal, eternal,
everlasting, imperishable and ageless.
You are not something tangible.
Neither are you something gross.
You are the Spirit – pure, perfect, eternal and everlasting.
You are the nub of philosophy.
The philosophy of creation, sustenance and dissolution.
You are the Trinity in which manifest the three modes of material
Nature.
Freedom is your divine vibration.
Liberty your sacred aura.

The voice of revolution is deafening.
Does it sometimes make people blind, too?
Is it this voice that seems to have made us deaf and blind?
What is it that appears to have clouded our vision and judgment?
Why do we appear to be sucked into the vortex of visceral vengeance
and cerebral erosion?
Do the colors of ideology have a tendency of rendering our vision myopic?
Why have we begun to be stolidly impervious to what is befalling our
beloved country?
Why have we failed to identify the minatory tendency to which we have
been hostage?
What is it that has propelled us to look at everything from the narrow
perspective of ideological straitjacket?
Who comes first, the country, people or political ideology?
What is it that always forces us into the snare of political correctness?
Is it true that the emerging post-truth era of politics has devastated
our cognitive potential to the extent that we have begun to succumb
ourselves to a new version of slavery and slavishness?
What is it that deters us from identifying Judases and Bibhishans, bent
on destroying what we avowedly stand for?
What is it that has inspired us to promote and nourish inimical elements,
only to be a victim of those satanic forces' unprovoked atrocities?
Who is that Brihaspati edifying us into believing that it is the core
injunction of our Constitution that not only commands us to be lenient,

but also strictly enjoins to nurture and nourish diabolic elements – and that, too, within our own national borders, as far as possible - in spite of their inveterate hatred toward us, our country and the principles we fondly stand for?

Doesn't it, in other words, mean that the Allied Powers should have invited Hitler's followers and bestowed upon them maximum care and hospitality within their own national boundaries?

What can be the most vulgar misinterpretation of our Constitution's magnanimity than this?

Who on earth can deny the truth that any document that encourages inimical forces to infiltrate into the country and destroy its people, along with the values they stand for, deserves to be thrown into the trash can?

Without doubt noble souls that refuse to come under the satanic sway of evils deserve to be greeted with due respect and love, in keeping with our longstanding tradition, no matter how different their persuasions from ours. And this is what forms the quintessence of our Constitution.

Why did Arjuna, at the behest of Lord Krishna, destroy the inimical Kauravas en masse?

How did Churchill emerge to be an eternal hero of the West?

Is it because they did not see any difference between truth and untruth?

Or they treated untruth in the same way as they did with truth?

No, no, no, no, no ...

Certainly they were guided by some divine instinct that would always declare: Vincit omnia veritas.

America, your magnanimity and munificence have been grossly misinterpreted.

I don't know whether it is meant for glorifying you or for jeopardizing your fundamentals.

I have seen some people pledge their allegiance to the Star Spangled Banner at the time of being bestowed with the most coveted honor of Citizenship of this great country, on the one hand.

I have seen the same people raise their original country's flag when it comes to advancing their competing interests, unfortunately at your expense.

The ingratitude does not end there.

I have seen them ceaselessly obsessed with the interests of their country of birth, as if their nostalgia had turned into an impassioned principle of self-exiled life.

I cannot help but express deep regret for how you have been treated by millions of people, without any regard for your legitimate susceptibilities.

People who visit brothels gratify their senses, but don't tend to give much of a damn to the honor, dignity and future about the persons involved. Because their loyalty and fidelity lie somewhere else.

Brothel to them is nothing but a ribald rendezvous where they can glean as much sensual pleasure as they can savor, without any enduring obligations thereof.

America, I don't know whether or not this analogy can succinctly grok your endemic predicament.

While expressing my indignation towards ingratitude with which your magnanimity and munificence sometimes tends to be greeted, I seem to have been a bit harsh.

America, I believe, you won't take it otherwise.

And appreciate my prostration.


Humans – no matter wherever they are and what religion or belief system they belong to – are the corporeal manifestation of divinity.

They have every right to crisscross the globe without any inhibitions and hindrances.

They can explore the vast cosmos without being a bit perturbed about contemporaneous innuendoes.

They can fathom the oceans without applying a brake on their relentless quest for the unknown.

America, it is your strict adherence to this principle that has made you the greatest country in the world.

You have embraced entire human beings as if they were your own offspring.

Your love and compassion towards them is definitely unparalleled.

As the paragon of freedom and liberty, any attempt at besmirching your image could be part of conspiracy, both from within and without.

America, how can you be identified with a specific administration?

How can you be identified with a certain personality, no matter how powerful he might be?

As the epitome of freedom and democracy, you are always above politics and partisanship.

So-called power politics and cynical partisanship cannot contaminate you.

Sinister attempts at bolstering party interests at the expense of your majesty and grandeur is really reprehensible.

The Statue of Liberty that stands at your heart always calls for freedom, based on time honored norms and practices.

It is not there to incite cross border pandemonium in the name of humans' inalienable right to freedom and liberty.

America, you are tolerant, munificent, accommodative and co-existent.

You have a strong commitment to peace and harmony.

However, that does not mean that you are abjectly inert and apathetic, as to prevent potential chaos and destruction in your own homeland.

How can you remain totally impervious to the possibility of your own citizenry, soaking in blood at the hands of nihilist desperadoes?

How can you remain totally indifferent to the flagrant violation of your borders by destructive elements, bent on destroying the core values that you have always stood for?

America, I know, the conscious and much needed focus – that had already been long overdue - on vital existential interests on your part, has invited plethora of chthonic adjectives, both from within and without.

Have you seen the sun and moon, having been scared of some potential cosmic upheaval, ever change their course?

America, just like the supreme Self as described by the Upanishads, you are self-effulgent, and your form is unthinkable.

You are subtler than the subtle.

You shine diversely, and you are far away than the far-off, and you are near, too.

In the light of this divine reality, America, I always wonder why you cannot make yourself available in dozens of countries:

Where people every moment cherish your affectionate embrace.

Where they die for democracy and human rights.

Where they crave for rule of law and justice.

Where they hanker after equality and freedom.

Millions upon millions of people across the globe are desperate to come under your powerful, yet compassionate wing.

It is not because you are colossal, affluent and endowed with inexhaustible resources.

Great philosopher, Yajnavalkya, in course of his discourse said to his wife, Maitreyi, "Everything is loved not for its own sake, but because the Self lives in it."

America, entire world loves you because the Self:

That sees God in every human being;

That finds divinity in everything, from atom to the universe;

That identifies itself with the Supreme Purusha;

That is radiant with immense power and puissance;

That sees the quest for divinity in each and every human endeavor that bolsters our civilization;

That wields the cosmic potential to vanquish evil, no matter how gigantic and powerful;

That respects every human being's intrinsic aspiration for peace and harmony, freedom and liberty;

lives in you.

Thousands of gopikas would always find lord Krishna with themselves.

They did not have to go to the Lord.

Rather He would be simultaneously available at all places for all of them.

Thus He would gracefully quench their thirst for His love.

O America, why can't you, too, reach them all, and quench their thirst for your love and affection?

America, wherever there is democracy, there you are.

Wherever there are human rights there you are.

Wherever there is rule of law there you are.

Wherever there is justice there you are.

Wherever there is equality there you are.

Wherever there is freedom there you are.

Why not bless the people of different countries concerned with these time-honored, precious values?

Let them enjoy your presence in their own country.

Let them bathe in your grandeur in their own land.

Let them experience your majesty in their own culture.

Let them feel your compassion in their own religion.

America, just remember how you played the leading role in creating the League of Nations, United Nations, and several other multilateral organizations.

Just remember how you created a coalition of nations to liberate Kuwait from the devious grip of Iraqi dictator, Saddam Hussein.

Why not create and lead a coalition of nations with the sole object of spreading democracy and freedom around the globe?

Why not embark on a sustainable mission, with renewed vigor and commitment, to bring about peace and prosperity, especially in the developing world?

Why not initiate an effective crusade against barbaric tyranny, despotism and dictatorships that tend to thrive in massive poverty and ignorance of benighted masses?

Isn't it our responsibility, as the leader of Free World, to work for the economic development and political freedom in such regions as are amenable to satanic forces' heinous brutality, resulting in the exodus of millions of people as refugees.

How long can West sustain the infinite influx of poverty and destitution, with subsequent cascade of problems, ranging from devastative terrorism to pernicious demographic convulsions?

Look at the seemingly indelible line of divisions the issue of immigration has spurred among political forces, both here and in Western Europe, obviously making them susceptible to inimical forces' devilish machinations.

Maverick giants, like China and Russia, have slyly managed to exempt themselves from this debilitating encumbrance, thereby raising their maneuvering leverage vis-à-vis the West.

Neither do they seem seriously concerned about the fanatical extremism that is eating into the vitals of developed West.

Why should the West keep providing a benign respite to tyrannical forces by shouldering their inexorable burden?

America, I know your eleemosynary mission will have to confront a great deal of resistance from various quarters that, unlike you, view international politics mere as a zero sum game.

They might even try to undermine your initiative by adopting a host of strategies, including baseless insinuations and innuendoes.

You might even be accused of pioneering neocolonialism, aimed at subjugating weak nations, and shoring up your own 'imperial ambitions'.

But you need not be disheartened and discouraged from such disparaging remarks, as long as your intention is pure.

Meantime, you should not shy away from employing both soft and hard powers when it comes to advancing your mission, in the interest of the poor, destitute and marginalized across the globe.

America, be powerful, mighty and puissant!

It is nothing but power and strength that can only bolster charity and altruism.

For a nation, weakness is anathema and strength religion.

Don't forget to make the most of the cutting edge scientific and technological innovations and discoveries to make yourself strong enough as to cope with any challenge on the part of evil, rogue and satanic forces on earth.

Since you are the sole bastion of democracy and freedom, you are on earth the last hope of mankind.


America, you are full!

From you fullness comes!

Even if fullness is taken from you, fullness still remains in you!

O America, the only true Hindu State on earth, arise and awake!

It is incumbent upon you to shower the children of supreme bliss with wealth and prosperity, peace and harmony.

It is incumbent upon you to liberate them from the endemic curse of nescience.

It is incumbent upon you to safeguard them from the savagery of callous forces.

It is incumbent upon you to expose them to the ebullience of scientific and technological advancement.

America, to me you are a true Hindu State, because:

You don't believe in any caste;
You don't believe in any creed;
You don't believe in any color;
You don't believe in any race;
You don't believe in any ethnicity;
You don't believe in any gender;
You don't believe in any origin;
You don't believe in any ideology;
You don't believe in any religion;
You don't revel in superstitious and bigoted mumbo jumbos, and
You don't rejoice in ostentatious rigmaroles.
What you intrinsically believe in is Soul - the reflection of the Supreme Being – residing in every human.
You believe in the objective pursuit of Science, whose sole aim is to inquire into and highlight the essence of eternal verity.
You seek perfection in every human endeavor – 'yogah karmasu kaushalam'.
You believe in the Almighty that essentially defines every iota of the universe, as the creation of some indefinable, indestructible and eternal power.
You don't believe in the personification of any God or deity; rather you believe in Brahma, the impersonal Supreme entity, embowering the entire universe with his divine power – all pervading, eternal, and infinite.
You believe in non-duality that sees in the entire creation of this universe, the reflection of the Supreme Brahma.
Hence your stentorian declarations: 'In God We Trust' and 'E Pluribus Unum'.
Intuitively inspired by the supreme philosophy of the Upanishads, you always seek truth through selfless service towards mankind and the universe that sustains us.
While serving the creations of God, you always put yourself above *raaga, bhaya and krodha*.
You seem so focused that no power on earth can make you veer off your chosen path, no matter how intimidating or enticing.

The victory of Allied Powers in Great Wars, along with the evaporation of the Evil Empire, reunification of two Germanys and the liberation of Kuwait are some of the stellar examples of your steadfastness.

Who knows, the 21st century might be the witness to your equally outstanding feats, when it comes to devising magic solutions in the interest of democracy and freedom, in controversial areas such as, China, Korean Peninsula, Middle East and Kashmir, to mention a few!

Certainly, there is no question about revanchist Russia trying to jettison itself off your prescient radar.

O America - the vivid manifestation of what sages and seers, like Yajnavalkya, Janak, Nachiketa, Barun, Uddalaka and Angiras had envisioned - arise and awake!

The world pins its hope on you as the unrivaled champion of democracy and freedom.

Mankind looks to you as the sole savior of its destiny.

Nation states find in you the selfless custodian of their sovereign independence.

You are the unfathomable philosophy of freedom and liberty, democracy and human rights.

In your enigmatic charisma is hidden humanity's eternal penchant for evolving into something, divine and reverential.

In your esoteric panache is shrouded the beauty of truth that has always mesmerized conscience bearers of human society.

And in the halo radiating from your divine persona is inscribed human aspiration to conquer perfection.

Therefore, America, arise and awake!

It is incumbent upon you to establish the 'Kingdom of God' on earth.


O America, the only reverential Hindu State on earth, it is your affection that has prompted me to speak the truth.

It is your magnanimity that has inspired me to speak my mind, as an innocent child.

It is fearlessness - bestowed by your motherly compassion - that has prodded me to challenge entrenched belief and tradition, and declare at the top of my voice that you are truly a Hindu State.

By saying so, I am not likening you to some execrable theocracy.

I am not trying to identify you with reprehensible fanaticism and bigotry.

I am not trying to undermine your grandeur and glory, radiating like sun in the universe.

I am not trying to offend your exceptionally admirable inclusive character.

Rather, by defining you as a Hindu State, I am trying to uncover the truth that had till now remained obscured.

Just like the face of truth is concealed by a golden vessel, do you, O America, reveal your true character to be seen by the entire world.

The day will come when my *prana* will be integrated into the vast space, and my physical body reduced to ashes.

At that very moment of reckoning, O America, what shall I have to remember, if I now consciously fail to speak the truth?

Therefore, O paragon of freedom and liberty, pray allow me to reveal the truth.

I know I am a bard - weird, absurd and eccentric.

I don't care whether anyone likes my outbursts and outpourings or not.

However, I am sure about one thing:

Time will certainly appreciate my love for fellow humans.

Time will applaud the greatest philosophy in my poems.

Time will admire the greatest beauty in my poems.

Time will commend the greatest music in my poems.

Time will esteem the greatest art in my poems.

Time will extoll the greatest literature in my poems.

Time will praise the greatest science in my poems.

Since I am avowedly committed to humans and humanity, time can ill afford to ignore the precious attributes of my signature.

That is why I want to see the beauty that no one had ever seen before.

I want to sing the song that no one had ever sung before.

I want to write a poem that no one had ever written before.

I want to envision a world that no one had ever contemplated before.

I want to think of something that no one had ever dreamt of before.

Truly speaking, I want to live a life that no one had ever lived before.

I want to die a death that no one had ever died before.

I am obsessive about my search for religion that helps me realize my Self.
That encourages me to make strides in my life.
That helps me grapple the intricate complexities of life.
That inspires me to give life to the dying.
That prods me to provide food and shelter to the destitute.
Above everything else, that helps me safeguard and promote freedom
and liberty of myself and that of my fellow beings.
I always appreciate meditation and accompanying practices when it
comes to enlightening our Self.
What good is religion if it cannot safeguard your freedom and liberty?
What good is religion if it cannot promote your existence?
What good is religion if it cannot shepherd your culture?
What good is religion if it cannot protect your identity?
What good is religion if it unnerves you into submitting to enemies'
brutality and callousness?
O yogis and monks of Tibet, have you ever peered into your past in this
light?
Entire world appreciates your religious predisposition.
Your longstanding tradition of meditation is also equally admired.
But I fail to understand why your religion and meditation could not
resist the unspeakable savagery of Communist assaults?
Why your religion and meditation could not forestall the slaughter of
more than a million of your fellow beings?
Why your religion and meditation could not protect your cultural
identity from nihilists' invasion?
I really don't understand why you continued sitting in contemplative
meditation while barbaric atheists were trampling on your
independence?
You still seem immersed in transcendental fantasies, woefully
impervious to the rape of both your past and present.
What would have been the fate of truth and righteousness if Arjuna had
gone into meditative retreat, instead of facing enemies in the battlefield?
America, what would have happened to your existence if heroes like
Washington and Jefferson had embarked on transcendental escapades,
instead of waging war against the colonizing power?
Religion to me is not a sedative.

Rather, it is a marvelous elixir, potential enough to give life to the dying, and strong enough to give both meaning and purpose to our lives.

It is not meant for decimating our nerves; it must reinvigorate our spirit.

I always prefer Yasser Arafat's quest for statehood to the Dalai Lama's flight into exile.

Struggle is life and escapism death.

Why am I so much concerned about Tibet and Tibetans?

It is because I don't want any precedent established that weighs so mortally on the future of mankind.

Especially by those on whom humanity has pinned high expectation.

After all the world is but a family.


O America, how big your sky is!

Entire world can easily fit into it.

How big your heart is!

The whole mankind can feel ensconced in it.

How big your mind is!

Human race prides on its exceptional cerebral nourishment.

Still I wonder why Rohingyas have been subjected to callous 'ethnic cleansing', and that, too, at the hands of a Nobel Peace laureate!

Can't you hear the woeful call for truth and justice coming from the mass graves, strewn over the land of Myanmar?

O America, how can your conscience condone, much less tolerate, such execrable excesses?

Isn't Su Kyi's conscious connivance a brazen mockery of the most celebrated prize conferred on her?

What has consistently deterred us from decimating the murderous Assad regime of Syria that is slaughtering its own people by using chemical weapons?

The plight of Yemeni people is also no less miserable.

Why should they suffer the worst humanitarian crisis just because of alien forces' macabre ambitions?

Equally perturbed am I at the perennial suffocation facing the Iranians - heir to a great civilization - at the hands of fanatical mullahs.

Why can't their longstanding aspiration for democracy and freedom be materialized?

How come a bunch of theocratic fanatics can determine the fate of more than 80 million people!

Iran's ruling clergy have not only quashed its peoples' earnest penchant for democracy and freedom; they are responsible for the terror and violence in different parts of the world.

How can one imagine the fingers of such apocalyptic mullahs on the button of most lethal nuclear weapons?

America, you have already had the taste of North Korean despot's growing brinkmanship.

Look, how the brutal dictator of that Stalinist regime is threatening the security of entire world.

How his cadaverous approach to the principles of Free World is tethered to his steady acquisition of Weapons of Mass Destruction!

Therefore, America, you can be anything but weak and complacent.

How can a weak nation face the demonic powers that overtly believe in the doctrine of 'galactic cannibalism'?

Once you become weak and inert, you will find yourself devoured.

America, you were not born to serve as delectable snacks for some ravenous Bear, Dragon, Pig or Porcupine.

Rather you were born to bless mankind with democracy, freedom and liberty.

You can't even imagine the diminution of these values by submitting to their portentous designs, aimed at stripping humans of their inalienable rights.

Therefore, America, arise and awake!

Make yourself strong enough as to extirpate the demonic forces that tend to thrive in the suppression of human conscience.

Make yourself strong enough as to destroy the macabre designs, aimed at bringing human race under the poisonous sway of bigotry, fanaticism and extremism.

Make yourself strong enough as to eliminate the entire forces that are bent on subjecting humans to hellish slavishness.

America, the last bastion of freedom and liberty, even if you equip yourself with the enormous lethal power, akin to the one, produced by two gigantic galaxies' violent collision, I don't really care.

Because I staunchly believe in your impeccable bonafides.

You will use your unparalleled power not for self-aggrandizement; rather you will utilize it for liberating human race from the most ominous death traps of autocrats, dictators, despots and tyrants.

And as per solemn injunctions of the divine providence, you will bless entire mankind with their most coveted dreams - freedom and liberty.

America, I am stunned at the way you have been sucked into the vortex of recriminations and name calling.

Pernicious partisanship is allowed to define your body politic.

Unfortunately, some elements - most probably, at the behest of some alien forces, wittingly or unwittingly - seem bent on destroying the fundamentals, underlining your conduct, character and behavior.

Their malicious pursuit subscribes to the conspiratorial design of inimical forces that want to see you completely torn asunder from within.

This is what explains the convulsions that our society has begun to experience in the name of race, religion and ethnicity.

Even a sizable section of the intelligentsia appears to have come under their diabolic spell.

I really feel pity for them who seem pathologically inclined toward kissing untruth.

Who is responsible for the recurring assaults on our honorable institutions?

Even the most venerable institution of Presidency does not seem immune to their lethal conspiracy.

To them the institution of Presidency has been the object of utter indignation and reproach.

Why do we fail to understand that once elected by the American people the President himself, irrespective of his party affiliation, represents the highest institution.

Going beyond the constitutional parameter to excoriate him as someone who has lost mental stability - without any substantial evidence provided by authorities concerned - might certainly raise the possibility of accusers themselves being leveled as unhinged, at best.

America, is it a crime to enhance your best interests?

Is it a crime to bolster your security?

Is it a crime to guarantee a bright future for the American people?

Is it a crime to safeguard Americans from enemies' attacks?
Is it a crime to strive for your prosperity and wellbeing?
Driven by vested interests, political opposition sometimes tends to
morph into lethal vindictiveness, with utterly hideous visage.
It does not behoove any responsible forces of society to succumb to such
meanness.

As a bard of the present, I cannot gloss over the issues that impact the
future of this nation, and the world.
I cannot keep wallowing in the world of fantasies, with complete
disregard for what is happening in the world of mankind.
I am a member of human society; therefore, I am committed to the
enhancement of each and every member of it, irrespective of gender, in
particular.
I cannot entertain any kind of standoff between men and women in society.
I have equal respect for both of them.
When the balance tends to skew in favor of a particular sex, I start
getting perturbed.
I believe in the principle of mutual respect and honor.
I don't want any women disparaged by men, nor do I want men
denigrated by women.
I am afraid impetuosity and impulsivity might sometimes drive a
wedge between men and women, resulting in the deepening of conflicts
between two sexes.
I do strongly advocate that the chastity of every woman be respected;
never her person be violated.
But women, too, should not be tempted to utilize the slightest pretense,
as a sinister subterfuge for damaging the dignity and honor of entire
menfolks.
O America, I know what I am touching upon is a lightening rod.
But I cannot help, because I don't want you to be condemned to the
potential hell of pernicious misogyny.
Mutual love, respect, honor and understanding must be the basis of
relationship between sexes.
America, I don't want your Soul squeezed.
I am afraid, it might presage a massive explosion.

America, I am always fascinated by your philosophical persona.

True, I am infatuated with the esoteric beauty of your Being.

The beauty that stems from rising above the body consciousness.

Your ideals have kept you from being obsessed with your own body.

Spreading across the globe, you constantly reverberate in the universe of human consciousness.

Just like clouds, thunder and lightening, born out of space, you don't have any specific shape.

Yet as a philosophy, you touch the transcendental height in your own way.

America, you might be surprised that I read the Upanishads on your glowing visage.

Sure, you cannot be realized through discourse, nor through the intellect.

Not even through the study of entire Scriptures can you be realized.

Just like the Self reveals itself to the one who desperately hankers after it, so do you reveal yourself to those who are earnestly devoted to your divine persona.

It is not possible for charlatans and impostors to realize the intrinsic essence, hidden behind your celestial splendor.

You are not only beyond the reach of the weak, but also imperceptible for those who are inured to wallowing in flawed discipline and practices.

You are above rites, rituals, customs and traditions.

You can be realized only by those who dare challenge the status quo and plunge into the realm of the unknown.

One can find you in the innovation, invention and discovery of scientific truths.

One can find you in the continuum, underlying the history of human civilization.

One can find you in the infinity, characterizing the beauty of cosmos.

One can find you in the mystery, hidden behind creation.

One can find you in the enigma, surrounding the definition of God.

One can find you in the ever-expanding nature of the universe.

One can find you in the subtlety of sympathy and the prowess of power.

America, wherever there is truth and righteousness, freedom and liberty, there you are.

Because you are essentially none other than truth and righteousness, freedom and liberty.
You are the greatest philosophy, on the thread of which are woven past, present and future of mankind.
The most reverential philosophy of freedom and liberty.

As a bard given to speaking the truth, I need to be protean, depending on circumstances.
Sometimes, I play a politician, par excellence.
Sometimes, I play a philosopher, standing in rank with Ved Vyas, Socrates, and the Buddha.
Sometimes, I play a scientist as consummated as Galileo, Newton and Einstein.
Sometimes, I play a poet extraordinaire, challenging even the skill and expertise of Kalidas, Homer, Virgil and Shakespeare.
Beneath this seemingly clownish theatrics is always hidden my insatiable penchant for seeking truth.
Because no politician is greater than truth.
No philosopher is greater than truth.
No scientist is greater than truth.
And no poet is greater than truth.
They are all seekers of truth, not the other way around.
Truth does not necessarily accompany them, rather they have to pursue the former.
Truth has an inbred aversion to even the slightest inclination towards its anti-thesis, untruth.
Truth tends to rejoice in the mockery of them who align themselves with its adversary.
Paradoxically by enabling them to receive the most covetous prize, award and honor.
This is how truth waxes humorous, sometimes.
I, too, enjoy savoring the beauty of truth's wit.

"Krishna, Buddha and Muhammad are not Gods",
declared a bespectacled pastor from the pulpit of a church.
"They are all fake Gods.

"They are not real Gods.

"Don't believe in them.

"Discard them all.

"They cannot bestow deliverance.

"To dub them God is to disparage Jesus.

"To respect them is to disrespect Jesus.

"There is only one God, and that is Jesus.

"Jesus is the only real God.

"All other religions are sham.

"Christianity is the only true religion.

"To pursue other religions is to denigrate Christianity."

If Jesus were alive today, how would he have reacted to it?

Would he have countenanced such preposterous outbursts?

Is that preacher doing service to his own God and religion by smearing Gods and religions of others?

Is he really serving human society by spewing such venom?

Doesn't it smack of bigotry and fanaticism?

How can one expect to learn spirituality from such broadsides, and that too, from a religious preacher?

I have as much respect for Christianity as I have for other religions.

I have as much reverence for Jesus as I have for Gods of other religions.

To me, all Gods and all religions are true.

All faiths and belief systems are true.

Peoples' devotion to their respective Gods and religions are true.

What really counts is belief and conviction.

Even idolatry is worth admiring.

Purity is the core of religion and faith.

Dedication in itself is always true.

That does not mean that I cannot pursue my own faith;

I cannot respect my own God.

But I don't think we have been empowered by any faith to hate Gods and religions of others.

Neither are we sanctioned to disparage pure faith and conviction.

America, the beauty of your Constitution lies in equal respect for all Gods, religions and faiths.

The greatness of your Constitution lies in allowing everybody to pursue their own faith and belief system.

The magnanimity of your Constitution lies in looking without any distinction upon temples, mosques and churches.

America, I cannot help but express pity for such soi disant preachers whose edification is nothing but the travesty of Jesus' holiness and sacrifice.

I cannot tolerate the sanctity of the Bible traded as some commercial merchandise.

Neither can I see the holiness and sacrifice of Jesus used as a poisonous nostrum, meant for desecrating the fabric of human society.

Religion and spirituality is something, quite different from clownish theatrics and histrionics.

Hollering, fidgeting, squirming and wiggling in the podium might entertain the audience.

I don't think it can help anyone realize the real spirit of Jesus and his great religion.

O America, I feel like engaging myself in a long conversation with you.

I really feel happy and enraptured at the opportunity my destiny has provided me to converse with Freedom and Liberty.

When it comes to fulfilling my eternal desire to dissolve myself in your divine effulgence, I cannot but divulge each and every vibration of my Being before you.

I wish I could keep doing this ad infinitum.

Why not? Because neither I die nor you, O Freedom!

Future is born out of past, and present always serves as a mediator.

As a dispassionate bridge between past and future, present has its own anguish and predicaments that it wants to share, so it might be able to relieve itself of their sustained assaults.

Present has absolutely no idea whether it was a dream or mere a hallucination.

An ebullient friar, attired in a ragged robe with blue, red and white patches, came to it.

Just like Socrates to some Athenian, O America, he began to shower present with myriad of questions, pertaining to you.

Interestingly, in reference to our own approach to human beings, humanity and the world.

Since never was present's conscience so deeply moved, it was desperate to share with me some of those questions.

While disgorging the friar's volley of questions, present identified itself with us, apparently in a gesture of solidarity, support and empathy. Present thus went:

Why are we always bested by others?

Why do we get swindled of by our own allies?

Why are our communities ravaged by crimes and criminals?

Why are tens of thousands of Americans dying of illegal narcotic drugs every year?

Why do our youths seek life in substance abuse?

Why are our borders violated by aliens with impunity?

Why are vicious gangs allowed to rampage our societies?

Why are we tempted to protect criminal elements from being brought to justice?

Why do we want to turn our country into a shambolic mess?

What has made us exceptionally sympathetic towards vicious alien criminals?

What has prompted us to flout the law of the land, only to serve the enemies of our society?

Why are we treating our legitimate authorities like enemies, instead?

What is it that inspires us to disparage and undermine honorable institutions?

Why do we tend to be so impetuous and impulsive? Why do we descend into pernicious recriminations and smear campaign?

What is it that always instigates us to be cynical?

Why are we inclined to take recourse to unbecoming broadsides and insinuations?

Who is behind our negativity that helps bolster our adversaries' machinations, at the cost of our vital interests?

What inspires us to drain our resources in the interest of adversarial forces?

What makes us virtually blind to the remarkable achievements made by our country?

Why can't we look at our beloved country, rising above party politics and partisanship?

Why can't we decipher the line between petty partisanship and comprehensive national interests?

What is it that prompts us to ride roughshod over the fundamentals of our Constitution and the US Declaration of Independence?

Why are we prepared to undermine the core philosophy of our Constitution in order to serve petty party interests?

Why are we so much obsessed with power that we want to achieve through any means, fair or foul?

Why have our representatives become nothing more than self-serving robots?

Why are they so impervious to the vital interests of this country and American people?

How come corruption and complacency has begun to percolate our institutions?

Why are our institutions growing effete and incompetent?

Why do we appear to have lost faith in time-honored democratic exercises, norms and practices?

Why are we inclined to turn our educational institutions into the training grounds of vicious political partisanship?

Why is our bureaucracy turning into a puppet at the hands of conspiratorial elements?

Why has our justice system grown so execrably biased and obstructionist?

Why have the media failed so miserably to serve truth?

Why have we been so vulnerable to psychopaths' lethal attacks?

Why can't we safeguard ourselves from radical terrorist elements, bent on destroying our values and institutions?

Under whose inspiration are we inclined to interpret the fundamentals of our Constitution, exclusively in the interest of our adversaries?

Why aren't we prepared to recognize the enemies that are intent on jeopardizing our power and influence in international politics?

Why do we choose to unnerve our own administration when it comes to negotiations with foreign powers?

Why do we always want this nation to play second fiddle to our petty interests and trivial ambitions?

Why have our politicians relegated themselves to third world demagogues?

Why are they twisting our sacred documents to suit their knavish dispositions?

Why are we eternally obsessed with race and color?

Why can't we sequester ourselves from obsolete and unscientific obsession with abortion?

Why do our family values appear so tenuous?

Why can't we pursue the basic philosophy of democracy, freedom and liberty?

Why do we hesitate to patch up mutual differences by seeking common grounds?

Why can't we protect our innovations and discoveries from being stolen by rogue states?

Why is the standard of our education on steady decline?

Why can't we be kept from being hostage to undue profiteering of insurance and pharmaceutical companies?

Why are we so meek and gullible when it comes to protecting our fiscal and economic interests vis-a-vis international competitors?

Why can't we realize that the decline of America will presage the domination of entire mankind by evil powers that tend to thrive in the decimation of human conscience?

Why can't we realize that the emaciation of our military power and clout will inevitably plunge human race into nightmarish slavishness at the hands of authoritarian and totalitarian regimes?

Why is our magnanimity being misconstrued as something, easily amenable to arbitrary contortion, aimed at undermining our existence as a sovereign, independent country?

Why are our thespians so much fascinated with the diabolic tantrums of partisan politics?

For all our commitment to their peace and security, why don't our allies seem grateful to us?

O America, present also recalled how the clairvoyant friar hailed Pax Americana, as the sole guarantor of liberal international order, based on democracy and free market economy.

Despite the episodic aberration - that prompted him to ask plethora of questions - the friar was fully convinced that Pax Americana will never cease to inspire humanity as long as the ember of penchant for freedom and liberty continues to ignite human heart.

Just like sun - the *prana* of the universe - rises and illumines our eyes, O America, arise and illumine the eyes of humanity.

You are the sole *prana* of this universe, and enormous power to illumine the world is hidden in your enviable commitment to freedom and liberty.

It is time to destroy the dark that is trying to engulf sanity and sobriety.

It is time to annihilate the dark that is trying to incarcerate probity and perspicacity.

It is time to extirpate the dark that is trying to decimate reason and rationality.

It is time to demolish the dark that is trying to unnerve our sense and consciousness.

It is time to bludgeon the dark that is trying to decapitate truth and veracity.

America, it is not that possible to perform this feat, without exposing the vacuity of established tradition and practices.

It is not that possible to effect any revolutionary change, without throwing down the gauntlet to obnoxious stereotypes.

It is not that possible to usher in a vibrant new era of 'We the People', without defenestrating obsolete impedimenta, associated with corrosive elitism.

It is not that possible to enlighten human consciousness without doing away with obsolete and anachronistic predispositions that tend to contaminate our vision and judgment.

It is not that possible to march towards vibrancy and loftiness without dispensing with rusty values, encrusted tradition and antediluvian institutions that are most likely to stymie our journey towards the goals, set both by science and spirituality.

Under your divine inspiration, O America, I wish I could write a new Gita. I wish I could write a new Bible.

I wish I could write a new Koran.

So I could give a solemn expression to legitimate expostulations, remonstrations, rebellions and revolutions of the Age.

Our Age seems to be replete with myriad of inconsistencies, incongruences, incoherences, imbalances and disproportions.

These all have made it suffer disorientation, vertigo, dizziness and even cognitive impairment.

Otherwise, I don't see any reason why humans should contemplate supplanting their own species with robots, especially for the purpose of happiness and fulfillment - something they used to obtain hitherto from the purity of relations with fellow beings.

I discern that our Age is asphyxiating with pent-up traumas, tribulations and agonies, stemming from our hackneyed adherence to rusty and rotten vestiges of the past.

Perhaps it is in dire need of an honorable catharsis that might even call for a surgical operation.

Time cannot remain static and stagnant.

It is ever flowing.

In its perennial flow smile purity and perfection.

The same purity and perfection each human Soul is radiant with.

When I look into myself, I find them trying to explode with profound imagination and ingenuity, creation and creativity.

The order of the universe is an unquenchable thirst.

It is an eternal search for something, new and novel.

In its scheme of things, nothing is constant, except for its relentless penchant for change.

Interestingly, behind its urge is hidden something unchangeable, immutable, eternal and infinite.

And therein lies the divine beauty of our Soul.

Despite being absolutely immutable, human Soul is unceasingly predisposed to expansion and immanence.

This is what inspires me to bring all human beings under my wings of love and affection.

This is what inspires me to share my joy and happiness with them.

This is what inspires me to ultimately emerge one with them.

I wish I could usher in a new era of peace and harmony, love and compassion, and cooperation and coexistence among human beings, by creating new scriptures and new holy books.

I wish I could be the Messiah with extraordinary power and will to purge our Age, along with beloved mankind, of innumerable inflictions, meted out by errant destiny.

O America, sometimes I think I am not writing a book.

Rather I am trying to build a dam of my thoughts, so I can regulate my effusive love and affection towards fellow beings.

O my fellow beings, I want my love and affection to be focused on you, and only you.

I don't want them to be dispersed and dissipated.

I don't want them to be unruly, and thus violate the idyllic landscape of your propitious existence.

What I want is to meticulously rear and nurture your Soul where I find my own sacred Being.

My fellow beings, I have an eternal relation with you.

I used to be your relation in the past.

I am your relation now at present.

I will never cease to be your relation in future.

My relation to you is based on the immortality of Self.

My relation to you is based on the eternity of Self.

My fellow beings, I am not only related to you.

I am related to each and every object of the universe, no matter whether they are animate or inanimate.

I am closely related to Nature, too.

As per the need of the hour, I do manifest myself with the help of Nature.

Both Nature and evolution sing praise of the camaraderie with my Soul.

I have been eternally engaged in this process, and I have always found inseparable soulmates in you.

I have always been as much enraptured by your prosperity and happiness as I am saddened by your suffering and tribulations.

Your vigor and enthusiasm have always enlivened me.

I reside in your Soul and smile at your divinity.

Many a time, it has so occurred to me - I want to write something, but I don't know what to write.

I want to express something, but I don't know what to express.

I want to think about something, but I don't know what to think about.

It all makes me embroiled in byzantine suffocation.

I feel as if I were completely lost unto some wasteland.

But my consciousness signals something otherwise.

Suddenly I find my conscience go berserk at the seeming paralysis of my spiritual mechanism.

Once I get yanked by my own conscience, I start seeing the world in a different light, even brighter and more soothing than before.

I find myself shining in the optimism of light.

I find myself smiling in the beauty of flowers.

I find myself calm and tranquil in the solemnity of the ocean.

I find myself agile and vibrant in the impetuosity of wind.

I find myself infinite and expansive in the infinity and ubiquity of the universe.

I find myself eternal and immanent in the eternity and immanence of my Soul.

# ÉMIGRÉ

Émigré,
Estranged from one's own motherland,
Suffering the loss of one's own Self.

Foreigner in an alien land,
Outlandish environs,
Strange behavior,
Constant victim of disdain.

No root, no tree, no branches,
Obscured past,
Blurred future.

Present intoxicated with
Enormous doses of hallucinogen,
Solitudes infected by
Nostalgic reflections.

Scorching sun,
Tempestuous wind, and
The all-pervasive snow
Questioning identity.

Treacherous footpaths and roads
Trying to machinate every movement.

Luxury radiating from posh vehicles
Constantly frowning upon
Unwanted, undesirable,
Gratuitous burden.

Life, an inanimate machine
Fueled by fatalistic inertia,
Incessant toiling,
No rest, no nap.

Workplace,
An innocuous gas chamber,
Constant psychological torture.

Love and affection,
A wild goose chase.

Successive enactments of legislations
Piling up of Damocles swords.

Émigré,
Like an explorer
Lost in the midst of the Sahara,
Looks to the distant horizon,
In fond hopes of rescuing himself.

# AN OSSIFIED MIRAGE

Amidst an idyllic ambience,
Adorned with the twinkling of stars,
One day,
Egypt's Pyramid overheard
The Sphinx murmuring
In wistful agony

"How can I forget
The days
We were together?

"Moments
We shared
Still haunt me

"We never cared
Disparaging comments
Wafting in the air

"Ours was a
Different world,
Exhilarating and ecstatic

"We were always
Under the aesthetic shade
Of spring

"There was no
Autumn to
Dishearten us

"Nor was there
Any summer,
Lachrymose

"The wind would
Whisper
In our ears

"Flowers
With their smile would
Cheer us up

"Time would experience
An amorous
Déjà vu

"Life exulted
With a new
Vista

"The universe, for us,
Was as light
As a feather

"We felt as if
We were blessed
With eternal pleasure

"One day
A massive earthquake
Hit our destiny

"The sun felt
Scorched, and
Oceans convulsed

"Because,
We had decided
To part ways

"We were not
Destined for
Each other

"With estranged
Destiny and destination
We smoldered

"Life turned out,
Alas! To be an
Ossified mirage"

Since then perhaps
Nobody has ever heard the Sphinx
Utter even a word

# GOD FLEES THE TEMPLE

Once in a December morning
I entered a temple
In the hope of
Getting an audience with God

But to my astonishment,
He had already left his abode,
For fear of being rebuked and humiliated,
At the hands of irate detractors,
Apparently in charge of inciting sectarianism

The floor of the temple
Was strewn with fresh flowers, and
Room profusely perfumed by
Exquisite incense

It seemed as if
Even the fragrance of incense, and
The beauty of flowers
Could not enamor God
From fleeing the temple

However,
Before departing
For an unknown destination,
God, in the name of mortals,
Had left a decree, scribbled
On a papyrus:
"Treating entire opposites alike
Is the key to enduring happiness"

Lying unattended in a corner of the temple
Was a decrepit idol of some deity;
Perhaps the only one
To honor the Holy injunction

# CRUEL IRONY

I get touched
by the beauty
of flowers.

My heart, as it is very
tender and delicate,
is liable to infliction.

Many a time,
it has been bruised
and lacerated
by profound
love and affection.

A cruel irony.

# HE WAS NOWHERE

With existence
steadily maimed and mutilated
by endless violence, torture and terror,
I sought refuge in the Almighty.

But alas! He was nowhere
to respond to my plaintive groaning.

I was shockingly stunned
when I suddenly found Him
prostrating before the lunatic
bigotry of pandas and clerics.

# THE WORLD CEASES TO EXIST

I see a deep sea
In your eyes,
Although
They are mountains
Of ethereal pleasure.

Every jot of your body
Is for me,
An exquisite aphrodisiac,
Exuding eternal ecstasy.

Your passions,
However spasmodic
And unpredictable,
Pierce into my senses,
Rendering me intoxicated
With attachment to life.

I see no darkness;
Neither do I see the light.
Entire cosmos turns out
To be an ethereal revelry.

Verily,
The world before me
Ceases to exist.

# VISITING A TEMPLE

When I visit a temple,
I get tempted
To dive deep
Into my own Being.

I try to find the difference
Between myself and God,
My inquisitiveness
Inspires me to question
His omnipresent authority.

I can't help
Challenging him,
When it comes to
Living a human life.

It is something different and uncanny
To influence mortals,
Being confined to a temple,
Or an archaic piece of stone.

Silence,
An eternal inheritance,
Supposedly forms the cosmic power
Of the Almighty.

I loathe silence,
A shield of the meek,
A devious cloak
To hide one's pusillanimity.

O God,
Arise from where you are;
Come out of the tiny closet,
And try to speak a few words,
At least about your own predicament.

I don't think
Humans are in need of your mercy.
Rather they are more than eager
To deliver you from your
Eternal state of helplessness.

# AMBITION

Ambition,
A devious entanglement,
That attracts mortals
Towards an inconceivable vortex.

What is greatness?
To respect or
To be respected.

Or is it a position
Wherefrom one can impose
Lordship over the mute and meek?

What is wealth and prosperity?
To die every moment for physical acquisition,
Or to share sweet melody of love
Among fellow beings?

Isn't ambition
A hallucination,
That feeds on its own illusion?

# HOMOSAPIENS

Distress,
Agony, and
Trauma -
Perpendiculars
Intersecting our
Linear lives

Emotion,
Passion, and
Desire -
Trajectory
Sapping our
Own Being

Rhetoric,
Gesture, and
Histrionics -
Elements mocking
Our existence

Homosapiens,
Truly, unfathomable
Horror of the Black Hole

# IT OWES ITS EXISTENCE TO ME

Entire creation of the universe
Is nothing,
But my imagination.

I am,
Therefore,
It is.

The moment
I cease to exist,
It disappears
Instantaneously.

The universe
Is but the function
Of mine.

I move,
It moves.
I spin,
It spins.

Each and every vibration
Of the universe
Is attributed to me.

I owe nothing to it,
But,
It owes
Its existence to me.

# MY TEARS

I find little
Difference
Between my tears
And waters flowing
Down the Ganges and the Nile

My tears,
Like those two mighty rivers,
Represent a long saga
Of human sufferings and woes.

Both the Ganges and the Nile
Were the pioneers of many a civilization.
It was under their affectionate embrace
That humans had learned to love each other.

But, instead of being grateful,
Over the centuries,
We have derided their fondness
By resorting to violence and enmity,
Just to satiate our trivial ambitions.

These days,
Both the Ganges and the Nile
Are mute and helpless.
They cannot enforce order,
Nor can they tame errant humans.

In the meantime,
They are tortured and agonized
At the sight of untold sufferings
Their offspring have been subjected to.

Just like my conscience,
Mortified they are
At gruesome atrocities committed
By humans on their legacies,
That once formed the foundation of
Glorious human civilizations.

Therefore,
I find little difference
Between my tears and waters
Flowing down
The Ganges and the Nile.

# DEATH IS NOT ALWAYS OMINOUS

One cannot see one's own birth,
But one can envision one's death.

Death is not always ominous,
It can also be propitious.

It can also be the beginning
Of an ethereal journey.

It can be a marvelous melody,
Flowing from the beauty
Of a full moon.

Sometimes,
It smells like jasmine,
With enormous power
To mesmerize us.

Death,
An enigmatic odyssey,
Can be the harbinger
Of a sublime destination.

# BEAUTY OF NATURE

Beauty of Nature

God's hagiography,
Written on the pages of wind

Sun, moon, stars and oceans,
Glamorous expressions of emotion

Flowers, streams and drizzle,
Erotic escapades

Idyllic landscape of blue light
Radiating from the full moon,
Caressing of the beloved

Fleeting comets,
Furtive glance of a nymph,
Vivacious, enthralling and effervescent

Floods, storms and hurricanes,
Expressions of ire and lividness

Earthquakes and volcanoes,
Revolutionary fervor

Torrential rain,
Tears streaming down
The cheeks of sky

Nature,
A celestial blend of
*Satyam, Shivam and Sundaram*

# MY SHADOW

My shadow,
I believe,
You are what I am.

You are my beloved,
You never desert me.

You are my alter ego,
But one thing
I don't understand:
Why do you try to conceal yourself?

Despite unflinching love and affection,
Why don't you caress me?

I have never heard you speak;
I have had innumerable moments
Of agony and torture.
You have never spoken even a word
To console me.
Nor have you ever expressed pleasure
In my happiness.

I have never noticed tears in your eyes,
I haven't seen smile in your face, either.

Why are you so stoic?
I am always troubled by your equanimity.

Should I take it as a sign of enlightenment?

If so,
Why don't you lead me
To your own world,
Devoid of the turmoil of opposites?

Shadow, my friend,
When will you respond to my eternal urge?

I have been waiting
Since the start of creation,
And I shall continue this journey
Till the end of universe.

# CONJUGAL BLISS

Tight embrace of sky
The earth feels ecstatic

The sky up, and
The earth down

Early in the morning
Sun smiling at their communion

Melody of earth's blushing, and
Sonorous voice of rivers and streams
Exhilarate entire creatures

All-pervasive greenery, and
Rollicking spring beautify the ambience

Nature always,
In anticipation of new creation,
Stares at the faces of sky and earth,
Both immersed in deep conjugal bliss

Amidst red throes of earth,
Every morning,
A new day is born

Ensuing celestial glow,
Paterfamilias' delight

# FRIGHTENING CACOPHONY

Frightening cacophony of Time
Hallmark of human destiny

Steady decline and devastation
Symbol of cruel irony

Life
An unending journey
Along the path of illusion

It is and it is not
There is and there is not

An esoteric juggernaut
Always loaded with nothingness

Death
An inexorable reality
Shrouded in callous apprehension

It is and it is not
There is there is not

An enigmatic applecart
Always driven by helplessness

# ABOUT TO BE BORN

I am silent
So is my conscience

Static is the universe
Ambience appears somber

Time is reluctant to move
Birds are singing poignance

Mountains are pensive
Oceans are calm

But the desert within me is smoldering,
And I am experiencing convulsion

Perhaps from the solitude of my Being
A new poem is about to be born

# I CANNOT FIND MYSELF

I cannot find myself unless I am lost

The destination of my journey is nothing but myself

I have lived thousands of lives, but still I don't know
What life is, and what I am

Sometimes I see myself in the tree
I find myself providing shelter to mankind

Sometimes I see myself in the ocean
I find myself absorbed in solemnity

Sometimes I see myself in mountains
I find myself buoyed by hubris

But they might be my reflections
Not my true identity

Still I don't know where I am
And what really I am

I am sure,
I cannot find myself unless I am lost

# I WONDER ...

Sometimes
I wonder if this world is
The product of
Some Shantanu's lust

Or is it an offshoot
Of Some Bhishma's
Unshakable vows?

Could it also be the
Amorous idyl of
Parasar's attachment
To blushing Satyavati?

Could it also be Shuktimati's
Profound gratitude towards
Vasu who rescued her from
Kolahala's putrid advance?

Whatever be this world
It is, to me, a mere reflection of void,
The ultimate refuge of the cosmos

# I AM LIFTING THE UNIVERSE

Just like Atlas
I am lifting the universe
On my shoulders

The steady expansion
Of the universe constantly
Adds to my burden

Even amidst the vast crowd
I don't find anyone ready
To share my pain

I can't let their nonchalance
Undercut my commitment
To the creation of the Lord

But I am not sure whether
The Lord Himself wants me
To hold on to this ordeal or not

# I HAVE BEEN CRYING AND CRYING

O Lord
I have been crying
And crying and crying
Since the beginning
Of mankind on earth

I don't know
Why You gave them
So much trouble, and
Unending afflictions

Deeply ached at their destiny
I have been crying; haven't
You seen these vast oceans,
The collection of my tears?

If you can't believe me,
Just take a moment and taste
A drop of those waters;
Like my tears
That, too, tastes saline

# I OFTEN FEEL LIKE RUMMAGING

I don't know why
I often feel like rummaging
Through the emptiness
Of my inner Being

Why can't I think myself
Of being something other
Than an interminable void?

Who is it that constantly
Inspires me to refute my
Own physical existence?

What object
Does he really want to fulfill
By impelling me towards
This amorphous pursuit?

Why is the galaxy of
My constitution so much
Attracted towards the
Supercluster of void?

Could it be my Soul itself
Or someone, challenging
My authority as the master
Of my own Self?

# O MY BELOVED MOTHERLAND!

O my beloved motherland, I don't think I am committing any aberration by deserting you only to embrace the whole world as the expansion of my Being.

I don't think it makes any difference whether I lie on your lap or somewhere else as long as I do identify myself with your eternal Self.

To me, you are not only the origin of my physical existence, but also the pious source of love and compassion, the only mainstay of human existence.

It is solely your spirit imbedded in my constitution that has encouraged me to explore the possibilities of recognizing my own Self in every individual on earth.

I don't think you should harbor any qualm when I solemnly prostrate before the living epitome of the divine spirit and values, that, as a land of reverential seers and sages, you have always cherished.

Who on earth can ignore the idyllic undulation of its divine beauty that seems to have permeated not only each and every atom of this land of the brave, but also the fragrance of its ambience?

O my beloved motherland, let me dissolve myself in the grandeur of its magnanimity and the majesty of its valor, as a tribute to my abiding obeisance towards your eternal affection.

Verily, I am eternally indebted to you for having inspired me to internalize the divine pronouncement of the Vedas that the earth is my mother and sky my father.

# REVOLUTION

The revolution
Of my hunger
Hankers after the Sun,
A oven-fresh pizza
Served by the cosmic pizzeria

The revolution
Of my lust
Hankers after the Moon,
The intoxicating beauty of a nymph
Nestled by heaven

The revolution
Of my thirst
Hankers after the Ocean
The inebriating glass of wine
Brewed in the winery of amour

# TENDER LONGING

Amidst
Smoochy silence
Of solitude,
Someone knocked
On my door

I felt as if
Someone hurtled her way
Into the room,
Even without me
Having opened the door

Silently sat beside me,
And whispered into my ear,
"Do you really love me?"

Totally mesmerized,
As I turned to the amorous voice,
There was none, except my
Tender longing

# WHAT CAN BE MORE POWERFUL?

Struggle between
Rama and Ravana,
An eternal reality

Vibhishans and Judases,
Cruel reality of
Human societies

Untruth howls
Frighteningly

Truth couched in
Sublime serenity

Truth seems meek and mute;
Untruth maverick and valiant

Roaring clouds
Fail to yield

What can be more powerful
Than the silence of cosmic hubbub?

# SHALLOW, SHALLOW, SHALLOW

Shallow, shallow, shallow
Everything is shallow
From heaven to hell
Timid chorus pell-mell

Shallow, shallow, shallow
Everything is shallow
From infamy to fame
Vain ballyhoo insane

Shallow, shallow, shallow
Everything is shallow
From crown to huts
Vapid hubris nuts

# O TYRANTS OF THE WORLD!

Seemingly invincible,
O tyrants of the world,
Your death has already
Been sealed at the hands
Of those who can neither
Speak not complain against
Your atrocities.

In no time will you realize
Who they are, and why they pretend
To muteness and meekness.

Have you ever heard the Almighty
Blab even a word?

# HOW CAN YOU IMAGINE?

O man,
How can you
Imagine liberating yourself
Unless you
Liberate your
Faith –
That defines
Not only your
Physical existence
But also your
Spiritual Being –
From sleazy lust,
Fiendish ambitions,
And cadaverous inertia?

# O CALLOUS MURDERER OF DAMASCUS

O callous murderer of Damascus,
How dare you poison your own people?
Don't ever forget that perdition is in store for you.
You cannot get away with this heinous crime against humanity.
Yours is a future replete with retribution and comeuppance.

O ruthless tyrant,
Your savagery will not go unpunished.

O brutal enemy of humanity,
Your suicidal paranoia shows -
Just like Kamsa,
Prior to the birth of Krishna,
You must have already heard
Yogmaya's portentous prophecy.

April 5, 2017

# BUGS AND GERMS

Bugs and germs
Should not be judged
By their size.

They appear perfectly innocuous.

What is menacing
Is their tendency and disposition.

Termites, however tiny,
Can bring down huge mansions.

O America,
Beware of these wretched creatures.

Don't allow them to eat into your vitals.

# WHAT AN IRONY, INDEED!

Hitler, Mussolini,
Mao, Stalin, Saddam,
Osama and Zarqabi

Your heads, putrescent receptacle
Of death and destruction

Your hands stained with
Blood of the innocents

Your legacy reverberating
With untold savagery and
Unspeakable barbarism

Your history echoing
The groaning and clamor of
Innumerable children and widows

Your name and fame,
The filthiest scum smacking of
Unbearable hellish stink

Your lives, a brazen reflection
Of heinous crimes and callousness

Your speech, the grotesque
Cacophony polluting the universe

Your presence,
A nightmarish anathema
Causing horrid dread,
And dehumanizing terror

Despite all these infernal experiences,
What an irony, indeed!

You will all enjoy
The same hospitality and respect
As Krishna and Jesus,
Muhammad and the Buddha,
At the heavenly palace of
Yamaraj, the lord of Death

Perhaps this is
What the Law of Karma ordains
There is neither Good nor Evil
In the realm of the Almighty

There is only one thing
That determines human fate
In the so-called afterlife,
And that is power and prowess

Even Dharmaraj Yudhisthir
Was nonplussed
When he found himself
Amidst the Kauravas and their knavish warriors,
After his entry into the reign of Yama

# JUST BE FREE AND LIBERATED

O dear Poem,
Why do you worry
About unnecessary
Rites, rituals and customs?

Just be free and liberated,
Harbor no limitations and barriers.

You need not cringe,
Nor should you cower.

You are the idyllic expression
Of poignance, hiding in the
Deep recess of my heart.

In your ebullience
I find Truth revealed.

And in your silence
I find divinity spelt.

You need not pursue
Any tradition.
You need not follow
Any mores.

You are always fulsome
In whatever way you
Present yourself.

You need not care
About any reproach,
Reproof and ridicule.

The manifestation of
My own being,
You are always
Pure and perfect,
Regardless of your
Physical appearance.

Look at the innumerable
Paraphernalia of Nature –
Rivers, mountains, deserts,
Gorges, plateaus and prairies.

Have you ever found them
Confine themselves to
Any artificial constraints?

True beauty lies
In your unvarnished gaits
And natural panache.

Yes, sometimes
You might seem
Incongruent to some.

Can't you see the congruence
Lurking behind seemingly
Incongruent attributes of Nature?

# COME OUT THE CHRYSALIS

O man,
Come out the chrysalis
Of your illusion
You will find yourself
No more a wiggly caterpillar,
But a beautiful butterfly -
A unique creation of the Almighty -
Pure and perfect

# TRY NOT TO WEAN ME AWAY

Try not to wean me away from my goal
Try not to divert me away from my journey
America, O paragon of freedom and liberty!
Pray, help me withstand all centrifugal enticements
Now I don't belong to anyone but you and only you
Let me snuggle in your affectionate embrace
I don't have any recourse but you
I don't have any destination but you
I don't have any pilgrimage but you
To me, you are the vivid embodiment of freedom and liberty
Let me get rid of all past vestiges,
And devote myself to the spirit you have always cherished

# YOU ARE THE TRUE RELIGION

O America,

You are the true religion sans rites, rituals and customs

Humanity expects you to dismantle the obsolete edifice of arcane imperatives

And create a new vista of human imaginations and ingenuity

What is religion if not total freedom and liberty that makes individual realize his own Being?

O America, only in your commitment to unfettered freedom lies the possibility of human dignity and honor

# LET ME SEE

Let me see how my destiny plays out

I don't care whether I rise or fall,
as long as I have trust in my Self

I have no illusion
that the world around me
is nothing but a mirage
of false hopes and fake promises

Relations are just like rainbows
that you can perceive from afar,
but cannot touch

Wealth and prosperity are shadows of evanescence

Name and fame mere snowflakes of Time

Truth will reveal itself
when a fully-blown flower
dissolves into the soil

Perhaps only to be one
with the Absolute

# I AM ABOVE THEM ALL

Time, space, causation
Earth, water, fire, and air
I am above them all
I cannot be circumscribed by their manipulations
Nor can I be constrained by their shenanigans
I am even immune to Nature's coquetry
Unfathomable cosmos is my playground where I play seesaw with destiny,
And fate is my valet, ever conscious about my corporeal penchant
Life to me is a romantic fantasy, and death mere a cathartic denouement
I am just a drop of water on the lotus-leaf

# VINCIT OMNIA VERITAS

Time is too powerful to remain incarcerated
Black clouds mourn their own demise with thunderous cry and
torrential pouring,
And the sky reveals itself - azure, abyssal and pristine
An invisible hand conjures up a series of cycloramas, involving
undulating waves of life and death
Histrionics, theatricals and gesticulations define our mortal existence
The amplitude of our dispositions vainly tries to defy the nature of reality
Time asserts itself once the ambience dissolves into plangency
Even the shadow of Time declares –
*Vincit omnia veritas*

# PYONGYANG IS DESPERATE

When human destiny descends into plangency, Time intervenes
As if to salve humanity it manifests, sometimes as *Kurmavatar*, and at
other times as *Nrisinghavatar, Barahavatar, Ramavatar*, and so on
It does project its cosmic power through various manifestations when
challenged to uphold truth, justice and righteousness
It does not even hesitate to perform ablution with the blood of evil
However hideous, Hiroshima and Nagasaki represented inexorable
interventions of Time
Human destiny is wondering whether Pyongyang is desperate to get an
audience with the Raudraroop of Time

April 25, 2017

# A WIZENED FLOWER

A wizened flower
Evokes no attraction
Have you ever seen
A humming bird,
Penetrate its long beak,
Into a withered flower,
With petals drooping forward?

# I DON'T WANT

O God,
I don't ask you
For anything
That you think
I don't deserve

I don't want my Self
Imprisoned even in Your
Mercy and condescendence

# THIRTEEN YEARS AGO

Thirteen years ago,
Today, we landed
In this most coveted
Paradise on earth

Free from the harrowing
Burdens of repression
And macabre uncertainty,
We entered the realm
Of idyllic exploration

Spasmodic nostalgic melancholy
Notwithstanding, we enjoyed
The new environ, fragrant with
Freedom, peace and hospitality

Life began to redefine itself
A meteor hurtling deep
Into the abyssal sky, as if
In search of something
New, noble and great

With freedom and liberty
Profoundly resonating with
Our benedictory conscience,
We did welcome the new
Journey - solemn and propitious

During the span of almost
One and a half decades

Not only the landscape of
Perception has changed,
Unimaginably poetic vista
Of destiny has emerged

The veil - however diaphanous –
Between the journey and destination
Seems to have disappeared,
And we have become one,
With the most respected,
Star Spangled Banner

May 14, 2017

# O MY FELLOW BEINGS!

O my fellow beings,
Come on!
Learn from me the eternal mantra
Through the chanting of which
You will be capable of transcending
Both life and death
Come on!
Look into my eyes,
A vivid manifestation of innumerable black holes
Through them you can divine
Even the last shore of the cosmos
Where you will find yourself
Schmoozing with your future
Neither God nor destiny can undermine
Your quest for something, eternal and infinite
You can see your past, present, and the future
Standing on the event horizon
Of your existence
Potential realignments and configurations
Of cosmic entities will ignite
Unprecedented divinity within you
Once you start waltzing
With celebrated cosmic behemoths,
You will find so-called saviors and deities
Woefully dwarf and diminutive
Your conscience, apparently consecrated
By your association with cosmic players,
Will make you feel exceptionally
Elevated and buoyed

# PORTRAIT OF TIME

On the cosmic canvas
Of Nature's silence,
I feel like painting
The most marvelous
Portrait of Time,
Behind the shadow
Of which will lurk
The eternal enigma
Of life and death,
With their carceral
Cycle attached to
Human destiny

# I FELT LIKE CRYING AGAIN

After a hiatus of several centuries,
Today, I felt like crying again
I felt like rocking the universe
With my blistering cry,
So even the mighty thunder would
Choose to remain mum and silent

I don't know why Prakriti was
So impervious to my sensibility
Why did she allure me into her
Carceral trap of lust and desire?
It is not my fault, rather it is her crime
To drag me into such a nightmare

Had the serpent not persuaded her,
Eve wouldn't have eaten the apple,
And she wouldn't have plunged
Into the maelstrom of mortal world
O my Soul, just tell me who you think
Is responsible for the fate of Adam and Eve

O Prakriti, why do you always
Play havoc with our innocence?
Why can't you allow us to remain
Pure, pristine, and unperturbed?
O my Soul, neither can I blame
Her outrage on your impassiveness
After all, you are my last refuge

# 'RESIST NOT EVIL'

I don't know
Why I always find my tears
Drowned in their own agony
They are meek, mute, and sheepish
They can't express themselves

They are prepared to endure
Any onslaughts, however
Cruel, brutal, callous and grisly
But they are not prepared to
Make any resistance

When I urge them to
Become vocal and react
To the atrocities of this world,
They further dive deep into silence

Irked at their resignation,
When I dare them to
Rise in revolt against
The harrowing brutalities
Of human society
They respond sotto voce:
'Resist not evil'.

# I WILL BE LOOKING FORWARD

O stars, planets and galaxies!
I am overwhelmed by your vastness

Even a brief glimpse of your immense majesty
Evokes myriads of questions in my mind

Even a slight touch of your magnificent presence
Sends unimaginable thrill through my psyche

I wish I could traverse your length and breath
I wish I could savor your eternal beauty

O cosmos, would you please allow my Being to be dissolved into your
immanence?

I will be looking forward to your kind response till the end of Time

# I AM NOTHING

I am nothing,
Neither do I want
To be anything

Simply, I am dust,
I want to remain as such

Position, decoration,
Award and investiture,
Nothing do I covet

Let me be reduced
To the subtlest
Possible level

So I can dwell
In the heart of
Fellow beings

As a divine Soul,
Infinite, eternal, and
Ebullient

# GOD BLESS AMERICA!

O my beloved America!

What has befallen you?

Why do stars seem opposed to your advancement?

Your own offspring seem to have forgotten your history, full of glorious pride and prestige

They seem impervious to your magnificent saga of love towards humans and humanity

They seem bent on besmirching your commitment to lofty values and institutions

Unwarranted saber-rattling among political forces has served to diminish your dignity

Sleazy smear campaigns have served to undercut your self-esteem

Vengeance and vendetta has polluted the psyche of elites and media

Most regrettably, even thespians have stooped so low as to contemplate only in terms of murder and assassination

O my God,

How horrible,

How bizarre,

And how grotesque!

Incumbent President's decapitated head soaked in blood - a perversion following in the footsteps of ISIS brutality - has been the hallmark of opposition!

Oppositional voice has turned into subservience to inimical forces that want our destruction

Obsequiousness towards our adversaries has been allowed to define the security and national interests of America and Americans

Oppositional politics appears to be synonymous with the destruction of values that America stands for

Instead of strengthening the foundation of our freedom and liberty, we seem prone to bolstering megalomaniac tendencies of fanatic mullahs, capricious dictators and scapegrace despots

We seem desperate to drain our hard-earned resources by bankrolling insidious forces' ulterior motives, latently aimed at jeopardizing our paramountcy

How shameful is our attempt at delegitimizing the reverential institutions?

In the name of exposing conspiracies, we seem spiraling down the morass of turpitude and profanity, much to the elation of our enemies

By resorting to such sinister undertakings, we are not only weakening our foundation, but also buttressing our enemies' assault on freedom and liberty

O God! What has befallen us?

What is it that has deterred us from coming to our senses?

If it persists, how shall we be able to lead the free world?

How shall we confront burgeoning threats of nuclear annihilation and fanatical blood-mongering?

How shall we enlighten the entire world with freedom and liberty?

In the name of mankind, I pray:

God Bless America!

July 15, 2017

# DEFINITION OF MY LIFE

O my Soul!
Please tell me
How I should define my life
Does my life have any boundary
That you want me not to cross?
How is its geography?
Does it evoke any interest in those who want to embark on exceptional adventures?
Does it have any history?
If so, is it strewn with series of incidents involving the gruesome slaughter of humans by humans?
Does it represent any theory of physics?
If so, how many Newtons, Einsteins and Hawkings have tried to fathom its essence?
Does it sometimes play religions that pretend to be the custodian of humankind?
If so, how many Avatars have so far been attributed to it?
O my Soul!
If you don't mind, may I please ask you a few more questions?
What is my life, a question or an answer?
Does it have its own language with different grammar and lexicons?
Does it also have the same subject, verb, and object style akin to that of ours?
What do its commas and full stops refer to?
Do they have any correlation with corporeal afflictions humans tend to suffer?
O my Soul!
Why am I so inquisitive today?
I feel inundated by myriad questions that, I believe, none but you can answer.

Are arrogant mountains the definition of my life?
Or the solemn oceans?
Why can't unruly wind be the definition of my life?
Is it because it does not comply with your injunctions?
Are you also a passionate aficionado of subservience?
Anyway, I don't want to veer off my charted course, because I am being accosted by Time, maybe for some important reasons.
Please tell me, O my Soul!
Is the definition of my life as vast as the cosmos and as deep as oceans?
Is it also punctuated by mysterious black holes?
Does it also occasionally experience realignments and reconfigurations a la our cosmos?
What do you think are the roles of so-called dark matter and dark energy of my life?
Do you think it is nothing but a tiny snowflake that disappears the moment it touches the earth?
Or is it the infinite power, the true mainstay behind the existence of this cosmos?
Is philosophy mere a lunatic fantasy, religion a fanatic pursuit for my life?
Do they have any bearing on my life?
It might sound somewhat awkward to you, but still I can't help asking you.
Do you find Vyasa and Shukadev somewhere in the definition of my life?
Do you think that the leverage of those sages' presence can weigh heavily on the direction of my life's definition?
Could you please divine the influence of Parasar's lustful attachment to Matsyagandha on the definition of my life?
Is it possible that Nachiketa's poignant transport, at some point, could liquefy the definition of my life?
Could it also be that Socrates' unyielding quest for truth will transmogrify my life's definition into something, abstract and inscrutable?
Do you think behind the definition of my life lurks Hubble's telescope through which mankind can peer into its destiny?
Does the definition of my life have an atavistic tendency of reveling in amatory fantasies?

Does the definition of my life descend into infatuation at the sight of divine union between Purusha and Prakriti?

Have you ever seen the definition of my life rise in revolt against tyranny and injustice?

How do you think it appreciates the sanguinary sagas of Hitler, Mussolini, Stalin and Mao?

Does it see any aesthetic value in my love towards fellow beings?

How do you think it will react to my indignation towards hoary and obsolete rites, rituals, customs and traditions that tend to vitiate the true essence of all religions?

What would be its approach to my equal reverence for all prophets and Gods that never get engaged in any undertakings, with the potential of undermining humans and humanity?

Do you think it will agree with my position that humans created Gods, not the other way around?

Will it harbor any reservation about my passionate plea that God is nowhere except within our own Soul?

Do you get sometimes exasperated at the incongruence of my life's thinking?

Have you ever noticed megalomaniac streak in its approach to contemporary international politics and dwindling world order?

Have you ever detected any anomaly in its fervent attempt at fusion between politics and religion?

Do you agree with its view that Krishna, Jesus and Muhammad were politicians par excellence, who were exceptionally adept at providing a divine veneer to their extraordinary revolutionary fervor?

Do you also agree with it that they had not established any new religions, but redefined politics against the perspective of human beings' entrenched predisposition towards embarking upon the unknown, instead?

Why does it see morality and ethics change their colors to suit new surroundings and environs?

Don't you ever subscribe to its take that no religions, however subtle and esoteric, can transcend the overarching boundary of physics?

Isn't it physics, and only physics, that ultimately leads religions and spirituality to fruitive conclusion?

What would be your reaction to its observation that true religion is physics shrouded in darkness of ignorance and physics religion illumined by the effulgence of knowledge?

Don't you think that the journey of religion desperately hankers after an idyllic rendezvous with science?

O my Soul!

What is the source of all knowledge, if not the abyssal depth of your enigmatic persona?

Therefore, O my Soul! Pray enlighten me, so I can encounter the challenge of time, with my divinity intact.

# AN ETERNAL RITUAL

A morning pregnant with optimism and myriads of opportunities
Sun purveying the brightness of our karma
Birds and numerous creatures of Lord engaged in their routine chores
Ambience perfumed by the ethereal spirit of Nature's dramatis personae
Man seeking his role in Time's cosmic scheme of things
An eternal ritual defining our relationship with the Supreme Entity

# CRUEL REALITIES OF DESTINY

Cruel realities of destiny
Sneaking into our life
Despair and despondence assaulting on our psyche
Summer sky streaked with saturnine lightning
Deafening thunders sounding dreadful alarms
Peace of mind inundated by swelling anguish
Calm and silence cringing at the slightest peeking of premonition
Harrowing shadow of death looming large
Still these are nothing but an evanescent flash of nightmare
O my Soul,
How can I be defeated
While I see you smiling at me?

# STATE OF THE STATE

Sate of the state
Nauseating and bizarre

An ambience shrouded
In malicious concoctions

Vendetta and vengeance
Threatening to devour
Principles and ideals

Inebriate media, jaundiced
Pundits, and anesthetized
Civil societies

Vulturine adversaries
Rapacious enemies

"We The People"
Bewildered and befuddled

Values and institutions
Suffering asphyxiation

Forgotten Founders and
Floundering Constitution

Politics synonymous with
Retribution and cynicism

O my beloved America!
For how long will you
Have to simmer like this?

July 15, 2017

# I OFTEN QUESTION MYSELF

Especially,
when I am alone,
I always wonder
if we really get vanished
in the abyssal wilderness of afterlife
or we shall be landing in some distant planet,
across billions of galaxies,
exclusively meant for providing refuge for 'immortal souls'.
I often question myself if I will
be able to find an answer to this
mystery some day
or I will have to depart without the Truth being revealed.

# HOW DARE YOU ...?

O my destiny,
How dare you expect
Me to grovel before you?
Don't ever try to cower me
I don't think I owe you anything
Rather, you owe me something,
Eternal, infinite and absolute

# JUST CREATE SOMETHING

O man, create something
Create something
Try to be creative
You can see God in your creation
You can see yourself bloom in your creation
Create something whatever you can
Creation has no boundary
Creation itself has no size and shape
Neither does it have any limitation
You can create anything from faith to God
From tiny robots to highly sophisticated spacecraft
From minor needle to state of the art supercomputer
Just create something, just create and create
Don't ever waste your life, wading in indolence, inertia and apathy
You have always remained the source of creation
You have always been the inspiration behind each and every discovery
You have always embellished the legacy of humanity by creating
something marvelous
Unlimited power of creation is hidden somewhere within you
You have been endowed with unfathomable imagination
Therefore, O man, don't be lazy
Realize your immense potential,
And create something
Your existence smiles at your creation
You will see in your creation the ebullience of your divinity
O man, don't let go even of a second
Create something, just create and create and create

# MAY I EXPECT YOU ...

An abrupt burst of happiness,
A sudden explosion of elation
Adding idyllic flavor to the beauty of a nubile blonde,
Enhancing the amorous charm of newly resuscitated Assembly Square
Who could have ignored the hypnotic power of amatory fragrance,
exuding from her lissome persona?
I wonder what might have inspired Nature to bloom through her
paroxysmal ecstasy
As if the full moon, with intoxicating luster, had furtively peeked out her
veil of clouds
I wish her exultation had permeated the world of beleaguered mankind
Her presence could have eliminated the agonizing darkness of our
melancholy,
And catapulted humanity to a new high of joy and loftiness
O lady, the paragon of beauty and fragrance,
May I expect you to ignite the divinity of human senses?

# I PROPOUND THE RELIGION OF MASS AND ENERGY

I propound the religion of mass and energy
I expound the philosophy of speed and velocity
I construct the temples and churches of physics
I build the mosques and monasteries of hospitals
I create pilgrimages of schools and universities

To me, cosmos is the sacrificial fire,
Unto which I pour the oblation of science
With the ladle of technology and database

To me, the cosmos is Brahma
The oblation I pour is Brahma
The ladle I use is Brahma, and
Of course, I myself am Brahma

And Brahma is the destination
Where I can dissolve myself
Into the Soul of humanity

# O STAR SPANGLED BANNER!

O Star Spangled Banner!
O sacred symbol of this great country!
You carry the glorious history of sacrifice and chivalry
Undulating beauty of civilization is embedded in you
You represent the highest spirit of America and its great people
You embody human beings' eternal penchant for freedom and liberty
You have always remained the undying source of our strength
You inspire equality, justice and brotherhood in human society
We envision in you a world of peace and harmony, cooperation and coexistence
To me you are the auspicious symbol of 'universality of spirit'
O reverential savior of humanity, may I express my deepest obeisance by embellishing your celestial persona with sacred Om!
Because I invariably see the Supreme in you

# I AM REALLY CONFUSED

The more I want to simplify myself the more I get complicated and esoteric
The more I try to avoid being abstract the more I get subtle and amorphous
The more I try to liquefy myself the more I get solid and ossified
The more I want to melt the more I get frozen and firm
Who is it that constantly weans me away from my own disposition?
And constantly conspires against conciliation between my Self and my proclivity?
Or could it also be that I have lost touch with my Self?
If so, how can I again establish my contact with my Being?
I am really confused if it is a question of philosophy or sheer nescience!

# CAUSE AND EFFECT UNTO MYSELF

The mystery of the cosmos reminds me of the esoteric complexities of my brain
The light of the sun reminds me of the most marvelous power of my eyesight
Deep oceans remind me of the unimaginable depth of my conscience
Rivers and streams remind me of ever flowing blood in my veins
Twinkling stars remind me of my incessantly soaring ambition to outpace Nature
Thunder and lightning remind me of the ebullient convulsion rocking my ingenuity
Black clouds remind me of my somber approach to aimless lives
Each and every component of the universe reminds me of something, relating to my Being and existence
But I have never found as of today anything that can remind me of my analogy to serendipity
For sure, I am cause and effect unto myself

# SOLAR ECLIPSE

Probably infatuated
with the radiance of Sun,
Moon tries to flirt with
the celestial hero,
and starts inching towards him

Although
consumed by reciprocal passion,
Sun does not want to embrace Moon,
lest the latter should burn to ashes

The more Moon comes closer
the more Sun tries to hide himself
into the dark

Finally, Sun goes into complete darkness,
and the seemingly jilted Moon
decides to veer off its amorous course

August 21, 2017

# AGONY

Agony
Invariably
Enlightens me

Lust
Occasionally
Tortures me

Fear
Seldom
Seizes me

Wrath
Never
Overpowers me

Imagination
Often
Captivates me

Life
Hardly
Nobbles me

Death
Never
Threatens me

# NATURE INTOXICATED

A land
Infested by dreadful demons, and
Bloodthirsty vampires

Mammoth congregations
Man helpless and alone
Terrified of his own shadow

Trees lumbering
At the sight of
Crumbling mountains

Far in the horizon
Sun munching on stars
Hummingbirds gulping oceans
A frozen moon
Trying to keep itself from dissolving

Wind with a broken spine
Desperate to flee the carnage
Hyaenas and wild dogs
Chasing rabbits and deer

A terrified ambience
Seeking refuge in the nest of a sparrow

Ravenous children with
Distended belly, engaged in
Scavenging foods

Charred pages of Holy Scriptures
Flying in pallid faces of deities

Religion murdered, and
Philosophy dismembered

Stinky odor exuding from
Rotten ideas and ideologies

Blood oozing out of
Impaled philosophers'
Austere bodies

Day cringing at
Night's reverberating
Guffaw

Dawn soaked in blood, and
Dusk asphyxiating

Lightening, smile of nymphs,
Trying to conceal itself

Thunder consoling the rain,
Suffering from dehydration

Far in a corner of the forest,
Priests,
In front of an altar,
Prepared from human bones,
Offering *charu* of human brain
Into the fire of passion
Chanting the Vedic hymns:
*Om Shantih...*
*Dhyouh Shantih...*
*Prithvi Shantih...*
*Aapah Shantih....*

Just a mile away
In the peepal grove
Nuns dancing naked,
Inebriated Buddhas
Playing guitars in ecstasy

Intensified libido, hallucinogens,
Nature intoxicated

# A SPLENDID CONFLUENCE

O solitude,
In your deep meditation,
I find both profundity of life,
And the eternal truth of death

A splendid confluence of
Truth, consciousness and bliss,
O solitude,
I find in you the mystery of creation revealed
You are truly the silent echo of divinity, pervading our universe

# IS IT MERE AN ILLUSION?

The quest for infinity
Has begun to define my life
The more I grow in age
The more I get disillusioned
With things mundane,
No matter how precious,
Everything, from tiny toys
To the crown, appears to me
Nothing, but a transient decoy
I have ceased to see fellow beings
In terms of corporeal relations,
But in terms of free spirit and an immortal Soul,
From whom I am no different
I can feel the beauty and bliss of cosmos within my own Being
I have begun to find myself established in pure consciousness
To me, my body is just a vehicle, bound for the journey towards eternity
I am wondering whether it is a preparation for Moksha or Nirvana
Or is it mere an illusion that tends to overwhelm many a savant?

# I AM THE SUPREME DEITY

A small temple I always carry atop myself
In it are Krishna, Jesus, Mohammad, and other innumerable deities
It's environ always gets reverberated by the composite symphony,
ensuing from different faiths and convictions
A vast cosmos in itself, it consists of billions of planets, stars and galaxies
Although an extraordinary machine producing deafening cacophony, it
is a calm oasis of order and peace
Most importantly, I am the supreme deity of this temple, not the other
way around

# ARISE, AWAKE!

Arise
Awake, and
Revolt
The world is yours

# ASK

Ask your
Own conscience
Who you are

# SOLE SOURCE OF LOVE

Along with
Undulating waves
Of vast oceans,
Flow my imaginations,
Carrying the message of
Universality of Spirit,
The sole source
Of love towards
Mankind

# THE SPIRIT WILL REIGN SUPREME

Sometimes, I feel, destiny has ordained me that I play John the Baptist. I pave the ground for the arrival of a new Messiah who will baptize entire mankind with the celebrated doctrine of 'Universality of Spirit'. The moment is not far when the world will realize the true significance of this philosophy.

It will create a strong and abiding bond among human communities by transcending the artificial barriers, created by religions and faiths.

Human civilization will again be reverberated by the eternal echo of this great doctrine.

There will be no caste, creed, color, religion, faith, and ethnicity to drive a wedge among human beings.

The Spirit will reign supreme, and mankind will enjoy bliss absolute, in their dissolution into the infinity of love.

# O MILLENNIALS!

O millennials!
Children of science and technology,
I appreciate your adherence to reason and rationality
I appreciate your relentless quest for the unknown
For your ingenuity and imagination, even the last frontier of cosmos is not far
Indeed, the cosmos is your playground
where you commiserate with the Creator, in a spirit of humanity
The more you advance, the more your faith translates into a scientific reality
The day is not far when your subjective personality will be defined in
objective mathematical formulae
Even your emotions and impulses will be defined in terms of geometry,
algebra and arithmetic
And your conscience will be preserved in a nano-mausoleum of computer
Your immortality will be an outstanding scientific feat

# HOW BEAUTIFUL THIS WORLD IS!

O my Soul!
How beautiful this world is!
Blue sky, verdure valleys, luxuriant landscapes, majesty of the
mountains, serenity of oceans, and expansive deserts
Sun and moon sharing their power and compassion with humanity
The vast sky bedecked with innumerable stars, planets and galaxies
Extraordinary order underlying the otherwise tumultuous cosmic system
Abyssal cosmos wrapped in the mystery of eternity
Living and non-living beings abiding by the wish of Nature
Human consciousness striving to cross the boundaries of destiny
Impetuosity of wind reinvigorating human spirit
Humans seeking eternal bliss in their own being
Mother Nature brimming with unity and harmony
Diversity adding to the fragrance of human existence
Incessant quest for unity vibrating human conscience
Unceasing effort to challenge the tyranny of death
Life everywhere blooming like flowers of the spring
O my Soul!
Thou art really great for having shared thy unique vision with me!

# THIRST FOR POURING MYSELF OUT

I don't have to please anybody
Nor do I have to disparage anyone
To me all are equal, and they deserve my love and appreciation
I write poems to quench my own thirst
The unceasing thirst for pouring myself out
The more I pour myself out, the more I feel fulfilled
Sometimes I am inspired by the forces of Nature
At other times by the affinity with fellow humans
Poems to me are the most convenient rendezvous where I meet my
fellow beings
I share my emotions as well as impulses with them
I raise the sublime issues of love and amour
Conflicts and war too, I don't hesitate to broach
While doing this, sometimes I get too obdurate and stubborn
At other times I get myself melted into poignancy and subtlety
Freezing and melting are two ends of life's spectrum
In between, there is a vast realm where I tend to search for poise
Beneath my unending desperation lies the quest for infinity
And that identifies me with my poems

# I AM ENTHRALLED

O Nature,
I am enthralled by your beauty
I can't express in words how you do captivate me
Each of your attributes vibrates my subtle nerves,
And I ascend to a divine realm of ecstasy
I am as much fascinated by your colors and fragrance
As I am infatuated with your beauty and music
I get enraptured by the sonorous melody flowing from your celestial panache
The moment I get transfixed by your nymphal languor,
I feel like questioning,
"Are you any different from my own being?"
Were it so, I would never have been so much smitten with you

# WHAT A BIZARRE CONTORTION!

The more you mortify yourself
The more I turn into an inanimate stone
Insensitive, indifferent and impassive;
The more you express love towards me
The more I feel anguished and tortured;
Vacuous, agonized and inflicted
I don't know whether this is love or something else
Were it love, why would it put me on the edge?
But there is absolutely no reason why I should impugn your affection
and kindness
Still I can't help suspecting
Perhaps I am clear about one thing
You love yourself more than you love me
That is why you don't care about my travails
And continue mortifying yourself
Maybe, your bizarre complex has some roots in your past
Estrangement and the feeling of being abandoned might have seriously
bruised your psyche
Maybe, you are seeking compensation for those times - spurned,
snubbed and scorned
You seem more obsessed with your lacerated past than your consoling present
That apparently makes you revel in seeking love by torturing yourself
But have you ever imagined the torture you inflict on someone whom
you claim to love more than you love yourself?
What a bizarre contortion of poignancy!

# HOW CAN I REDUCE MYSELF?

O God
I don't care
Whether or not the world
Relishes my presence
As long as you approve of
My existence, regardless of my
Caste, color, race and religion
I am especially thankful to those
Who are inclined to shun and ostracize me,
It is their indignation that most of the time propels me towards Your
divine embrace
How can I reduce myself to an execrable ingrate?

# ROAR LIKE A LION

O youths of the world!
There is neither heaven nor hell
These are mere illusion in which
You seem entangled
Hurry up!
Just come out this chimera
Let not Time fleet past you
Realize the power inherent in your Self
Arise, awake,
And roar like a lion

# KNOCK ON THE DOOR OF YOUR HEART

O man,
Why are you lamenting your plight?
Why are you groaning plaintively?
Even the almighty seems indifferent
Let alone your own fellow beings
Don't expect anyone to redress your travails
Nor can they do so, even if they wish
It is you, and none, but you who can only grant solace to yourself
What you have to do is knock on the door of your own heart
Certainly your Self, the great emancipator, will respond

# O AMERICA, I SALUTE THEE!

The inexhaustible
Source of compassion,
O America,
I salute thee!

The affectionate savior
Of human beings and humanity,
O America,
I salute thee!

The immortal embodiment
Of freedom and liberty,
O America,
I salute thee!

The greatest bastion
Of democracy and human rights,
O America,
I salute thee!

The uncontested Superpower
Of the mortal world,
O America,
I salute thee!

The puissant destroyer
Of evil forces on earth,
O America,
I salute thee!

The staunch advocate
Of peace and harmony,
O America,
I salute thee!

The passionate dispenser
Of equality and justice,
O America,
I salute thee!

The hallowed land
Of the brave and just,
O America,
I salute thee!

The enthusiastic pioneer
Of innovation and discoveries,
O America,
I salute thee!

The greatest champion
Of secular and pluralistic values,
O America,
I salute thee!

The ardent advocate
Of truth and righteousness,
O America,
I salute thee!

The greatest philosophy
Of freedom and liberty,
O America,
I salute thee!

The unswerving adherent
Of celebrated divine values,
O America,
I salute thee!

The compassionate protector
Of the dispossessed and distressed,
O America,
I salute thee!

The powerful custodian
Of nation states' sovereignty and independence,
O America,
I salute thee!

The great guarantor
Of liberal political order,
O America,
I salute thee!

The strongest advocate
Of the rule-based international order,
O America,
I salute thee!

The relentless pursuer
Of legitimate wealth and prosperity,
O America,
I salute thee!

The enviable center
Of scientific and technological advancement,
O America,
I salute thee!

The revolutionary pioneer
Of same-sex marriage and gender equality,
O America,
I salute thee!

The outstanding promoter
Of both religious and secular values,
O America,
I salute thee!

The uncompromising advocate
Of racial harmony and tolerance,
O America,
I salute thee!

The unprecedented proponent
Of the 'Universality of Spirit',
O America,
I salute thee!

The vivid embodiment
Of scriptures and sacred treatises,
O America,
I salute thee!

The venerable preserver
Of the immortal legacy of seers and sages,
O America,
I salute thee!

The true admirer
Of human potential and ingenuity,
O America,
I salute thee!

The most dependable supporter
Of international friends and allies,
O America,
I salute thee!

The strongest advocate
Of conservation and environment,
O America,
I salute thee!

The ingenious leader
Of the cosmos and space exploration,
O America,
I salute thee!

The greatest inspiration
Of literature, science and philosophy,
O America,
I salute thee!

The passionate upholder
Of human civilization,
O America,
I salute thee!

The sole guardian
Of humans and their sacred existence,
O America,
I salute thee!

The undying voice
Of humanity's urge for freedom,
O America,
I salute thee!

The unyielding guardian
Of liberal values and institutions,
O America,
I salute thee!

The ambrosial quintessence
Of all religions and faiths,
O America,
I salute thee!

The illustrious example
Of glorious human civilization,
O America,
I salute thee!

The exemplary advocate
Of celebrated family values,
O America,
I salute thee!

The most august land
Of bravery and sacrifice,
O America,
I salute thee!

The eternal source
Of elegance and munificence,
O America,
I salute thee!

The divine rendezvous
Of humanity and divinity,
O America,
I salute thee!

The wondrous land
Of realizing one's own Being,
O America,
I salute thee!

The marvelous mosaic
Of diverse ethnic communities,
O America,
I salute thee!

The visionary seer
Of unity in diversity,
O America,
I salute thee!

The most sacred land
Of 'We the People',
O America,
I salute thee!

The pious country
Of unimaginable power and strength,
O America,
I salute thee!

The trenchant detractor
Of cowardice and pusillanimity,
O America,
I salute thee!

The ardent champion
Of deep patriotic fervor,
O America,
I salute thee!

The vibrant practitioner
Of democratic principles and ideals,
O America,
I salute thee!

The idyllic panorama
Of natural beauty and fragrance,
O America,
I salute thee!

The unrivaled powerhouse
Of most dedicated and patriotic servicemen,
O America,
I salute thee!

The empyreal paragon
Of majesty and grandeur,
O America,
I salute thee!

The unique apotheosis
Of human perfection and paramountcy,
O America,
I salute thee!

The true admirer
Of human potential and endeavor,
O America,
I salute thee!

The great preserver
Of Nature and its sublime beauty,
O America,
I salute thee!

The passionate aficionado
Of arts and aesthetics,
O America,
I salute thee!

Verily, the most
Coveted heaven on earth,
O America,
I salute thee!

# HOW BLESSED THOU ART!

O man,
How blessed thou art!
The earth providing thee with a tranquil sanctuary
Fluidity of water constantly keeping thy emotions moistened
Fire rekindling thy ever-soaring spirit
Space reinvigorating thy immeasurable ingenuity
Air incessantly sustaining thy august existence
Thy mind always seeking the serenity of calm
Thy intellect unceasingly engaged in the exploration of the unknown,
And ego constantly reminding thou of thy unmatched position in the universe
O man,
How blessed thou art!

# WHY NOT FIND SOME BETTER ALTERNATIVE?

Sanguinary present sometimes pushes me to think -
perhaps Krishna and the Buddha have become obsolete; Jesus and
Muhammad anachronistic.

Fraught with destructive anomalies and debilitating inconsistencies,
their order has been reduced to terror, violence, superstition, bigotry and
fanaticism.

Is it possible to retain this order along with its devastating toll on human
lives and humanity?

How far is it worth it?

Why not find some better alternative?

I am always after something that is even greater than infinity.

I am always after something that is even higher than divinity.

Why should our journey stop at gods, prophets and messengers of yore?

Why not excavate some new phenomenon?

Reliance on the past could be the denial of present.

And denial of the present could be the destruction of future.

It is just one of the dimensions of our imagination that created gods and
divinity.

We are still endowed with millions and millions more.

We are infinite and eternal unto ourselves.

We possess the potential to create innumerable phenomena, as mesmerizing as gods and divinity.

It is high time that we contrived something new, benign, sovereign and supple.

And we pulled the curtains on this phase, akin to the eclipse of a Kalpa, followed by the birth of a new day of Brahma.

# GIVE THEM A DEATH KISS

O youths of the suppressed lands,
Arise and awake!
You are the future of this world
You are the inspiration of humanity
You are the illuminating light of hope
Be not scared of tyrants' tyranny
Never submit to their ruthlessness
Yield not to indifference, either
Tyrants and despots, dictators and autocrats are nothing but the effigies
of powder keg
Look, how vulnerable they are to their own brutality and callousness
Your courage and boldness can be the most potent ignition
Come on, give them a death kiss, and see how they burn to ashes

# SOMETHING APPEARS AMISS, MY FRIEND

Something appears amiss, my friend
As I have embarked on the twilight of my life, I seem to have failed to understand its language
Neither am I well versed in its grammar
Let alone savor the sublime sweetness of its literature
I don't know where I need to start from again
An undying craze for diving into its music and beauty constantly torments me
How about restarting from simple vocabularies?

# WHAT REALLY MATTERS IS TRUTH

Billions of people
Billions of approaches
Billions of perceptions
Billions of angles
Billions of dispositions
Billions of proclivities
To some, Krishna could be a sly playboy
Buddha a depressed derelict
Gandhi a casteist sex-maniac
Jesus an imagination of apostles
Hitler a savior of humanity
Stalin the custodian of the proletariat
Mao a bright star on the sky of China
It does not matter how people perceive
What really matters is truth
And truth does never change its color

# TIME IS ALWAYS NONCHALANT

Once you live,
Every moment becomes obsolete
You cannot relive it
You cannot stop the fleeting Time
Neither does it deign to pause for you
Time is not your relation
Time is always nonchalant
It's the illusion of flirting with Time
That gives rise to our ecstasy and agony
Even life and death are the gratuity of Time –
Condescending and sardonic

# HOW CAN YOU SUCCUMB?

O man,
You are an immortal Soul
How can you succumb to defeat and despair?
However arduous your journey, victory always awaits you
Nothing is more powerful than your silence
Neither is anything mightier than your purity
Drawing on these precious attributes,
O man,
March ahead, march ahead!
Victory is yours!!

# RAMESH, HURRY UP!

Ramesh,
Hurry up!
Time's running out
Don't waste even a second
You've a long way to traverse
However, be calm and persistent, silent and pure
Nothing can stop you from reaching your goal

# ETHEREAL DIVINITY

Innumerable imponderables
Wafting in the firmament
Of my idyllic psyche

Ineffable rapture
Profusely pouring
Out of my Being

Myself turned into
The exulted shadow
Of bliss absolute

Universe of my
Existence enveloped by
The romance of Adam and Eve

My heartbeat adorned
With amatory symbiosis
Between Krishna and gopikas

Really a celestial
Ascent into the world
Of ethereal divinity

# BETTER TO BE AN APOSTATE

If my faith advocates
Hatred and hostility,
I discard it.

If my faith teaches
Bigotry and fanaticism,
I disdain it.

If my faith exhorts
Violence and terrorism,
I denounce it.

If my faith relishes
The blood of humans
I condemn it.

If my faith destroys
The souls of fellow beings,
I incinerate it.

Indeed, it is
Better to be an apostate
Than to submit oneself
To satanic injunctions.

# WHY WE FAIL TO HEED

O my Soul,
I don't see any difference
between the Ganges and the Nile;
Neither do I see any difference
between the Indian Ocean and
the Persian Gulf.
To me, they are all sacred embodiments
of civilizational values, that have nourished
and nurtured humanity, irrespective of religion,
race, culture, faith and belief.
I have always felt the solemn vibrations of
the Gita and Koran, the Bible and Torah,
in their unvarnished confidence in human beings,
as the true messengers of God, built in His own image.
I wonder, O my Soul, why we fail to heed
thy agony, brewing from our base penchant
for saber rattling just over paltry ambitions.

# FAITH'S DEADPAN

Holy scriptures once
Complained: "Why has
Devotion become so
Cosmetic these days?"

"Maybe, peoples' confidence
In themselves has crumbled,"
Deadpanned Faith.

# BEAUTY AND UGLINESS

Ugliness once asked Beauty,
"Why do people get so much attracted to your personality."
Beauty answered, "Maybe they are attracted toward themselves."
"If you think so, why are not they attracted toward me," asked Ugliness
wistfully.
'You may ask this question to your own conscience," replied Beauty.
Obligingly, Ugliness asked the same question to her conscience and the
latter responded, "People are neither attracted toward Beauty, nor are
they repulsed by Ugliness. In essence, what they do is try to hear the
solemn melody, reverberating in their Self, through the prism of outward
objects, that to the Self, are neither beautiful nor ugly."

# HOW SHALL I DEFINE?

How shall I define happiness,
When my heart is so heavy with misery?

How shall I define prosperity,
When I am so steeped in adversity?

How shall I define the light of day,
When I am so smitten with the dark of night?

How shall I define the beauty of life,
When I am betrothed to the ugliness of death?

How shall I define myself,
When I have been one with all?

# THE MOMENT I SAVOR

The moment
I savor the poignancy
Of my own tears,
I morph into
The most beautiful poems,
Ever written by a bruised heart.

The moment
I savor the agony
Of my own life,
I turn into
The most ebullient experience,
Ever realized by human soul.

The moment
I savor the trauma
Of my own existence,
I dissolve into
The most cherished ecstasy,
Ever spewed by mother Nature.

# WHY CAN'T YOU TELL YOUR DEVOTEES?

O Krishna and Jesus,
Buddha and Mohammad!

Why can't you tell your devotees
That truth lies not in your dead bodies,
But in the live souls of humans?

Why can't you tell your devotees
That sanctity lies not in your earthly abodes,
But in the blood of the innocent?

Why can't you tell your devotees
That righteousness lies not in rancid scriptures,
But in pure appreciation of fellow beings?

Why can't you tell your devotees
That paradise lies not in the distant horizon,
But in the service of mankind?

Why can't you tell your devotees
That devotion lies not in mere incantation,
But in responding to the cry of human heart?

Why can't you tell your devotees
That emancipation lies not in your service,
But in sincere empathy towards fellow humans?

Why can't you tell your devotees
That martyrdom lies not in exploding oneself,
But in anointing the masses with love and compassion?

# HE IS HERE ...

He is here
He is there
Everywhere He is

He isn't here
He isn't there
Nowhere He is

You can see Him
I can see Him
Visible He is

You can't see Him
I can't see Him
Invisible He is

He is the melody of Nature
Serenity of solitude He is

# TORNADO AND THE MOUNTAIN

After having witnessed a series of
Devastations wrought by Tornado,
The mountain, with deep sympathy
Towards the victims, once politely
Asked the perpetrator, "What is their
Crime that prompted you to destroy them
En masse, and that too, so ruthlessly?"

As if provoked by the 'effrontery' of
The mountain to ask him about the
Crime of the victims, the roving tyrant
Of Nature tried to brush aside the
Issue with a brusque response: "It is
None of your business."

The mountain, as it was lofty not only
In physical size but also in its approach
To the entire creation of the Almighty,
In a polite, yet firm tone, persisted,
"Isn't it a crime to defy the divine order
By being so callous toward the innocents?"

With his eyes brimming with arrogance
And ire, Tornado, in a coarse voice
Blurted out, "If you keep interceding this
Way, I might have to launch a similar
Attack on you, too. Therefore, stop all
This nonsense, and get focused on your
Own business."

Fully confident in his own colossal power,
The mountain, with a streak of sneer in his
Stentorian voice, dared the pipsqueak to test
His strength by mounting an attack on him.

Overwhelmed by suicidal hubris, insolent
And impetuous Tornado hurtled itself toward
The colossus, only to be blown into tiny puffs,
Prone to instant evaporation.

Since then, Tornadoes, no matter how powerful
And devastating, seem to be extremely cautious,
When it comes to facing the majesty of mountains.

# I AM DEEPLY TOUCHED

I am infatuated
with the beautiful
color of present.

Past, to me,
is the instantaneous
evaporation of camphor.

In future, lies my
atavistic penchant for
the Resurrection.

# DESTINY OF TIME

"It is sown a natural body;
It is born a spiritual body,"
Said Paul while delving on
The spiritual journey of man.

The journey of human beings
Is a journey of consciousness;
From lower to the higher level.
Both the destination and goal
Can't be anything but freedom.

Therefore, O man, march ahead!
Your are the child of immortal bliss!
You are a free spirit, an immortal Soul!
It is not Time that decides your future;
It is you who define the destiny of time.

# YOUR DESTINATION BECKONS YOU

O man,
Your journey should not stop at Krishna and Jesus, Muhammad and the Buddha
Highly reverential, even these masters are mere means, not your end
You are destined to go way far beyond them
You cannot afford to remain stuck in any time, space and personality
In the course of your journey you have to create thousands, each of the Gita, Bible and Koran
You have to cherish thousands, each of Krishna, Jesus, Muhammad and the Buddha
You have to explore even higher ideals to better suit your Being and ambience
You are a relentless traveler, embarked on an infinite journey
Remember, your destination from across the cosmos always beckons you

# I DON'T WANT TO EVANESCE

I am not a king, nor an emperor.
Neither did I ever harbor such megalomania.
As a tiny dust of this earth, I always seek a rightful place.
Not only in human society but also in the cosmic scheme of things.
Though tiny and feeble, I don't want to evanesce.
I never admire the fate of snowflakes.
I want to bear witness to the eternal evolution of the universe.
I don't want to evaporate; I don't want to die.
I want to be the master of my Self, so I can manifest any time I wish to.
I want the universe to be a plaything at my hands - seemingly tiny and feeble.

# DON'T GET CONFUSED

Ramesh,
Don't get confused
You are both your journey and destination
There is nothing beyond you
You are yourself your goal
You are a traveler of an interminable journey
The moment you reach your Self, your journey will come to an end
And that will be the vantage point where you will find yourself merged
with the Absolute
The difference between you and the Creator will also disappear

# BE FREE AND ENJOY LIFE

O man try to know first, who you are
If you don't even know yourself, how can you be free?
How can you enjoy life?
If you fail to know yourself, your freedom might be trampled by
tyrannical forces
Just imagine how torturous it will be
Come on, know yourself
And protect, preserve and enjoy your freedom
Without freedom you are nothing, but a composite mass of inorganic
elements,
Prone to inexorable dissolution
Therefore, arise and awake
Be free and enjoy life!

# HOW DARE YOU EXPECT ME?

O my destiny,
How dare you expect
Me to grovel before you?
Don't ever try to cower me
I am not a helpless lackey of yours
Rather, I am the master of your fate

# I AM ENGAGED

I am engaged in seeking life
In flowers, rivers, winds, trees and clouds;
In earthquakes, volcanos, tsunamis, and floods
Everywhere I seek lives as vibrant and vigorous as I am
I see in all of them the beauty and bliss of Nature
I rejoice at their vivacity and vividness
They touch the core of my Being
And it dances to the tune of Truth

# HOW CAN I LAY CLAIM?

O Earth, the foundation from which I did sprout,
O Water, the liquid that sustains my existence,
O Fire, the element that has always ignited my spirit,
O Ether, something that has often shaped my vision,
O Air, the mainstay of my corporeal life and existence,
How can I lay claim to myself while I don't possess anything, except for
everything that I owe you?

# I AM SINGULARITY

I am Singularity
I am infinitely dense
Even the spacetime curvature cannot face me;
Therefore is bound to yield
Light prostrates before my omnipotence
Entire laws of Physics kneel before me
They find my infinity beyond their comprehension
I create the universe and destroy it at my own will
I am always a mystery; never to be fathomed
Billions of galaxies are nothing but tiny specks, paying obeisance to my
transcendental power and prowess
I am the Supreme, neither with a beginning nor with an end
Even the definition of God falls short of portraying my cosmic persona
Neither the theory of gravity nor quantum physics can grok my
immanence
Not even their unified efforts can comprehend the enigma, surrounding
my eternity
I am an ever-effulgent Soul, the ultimate identity of every human being
on earth

# WITH SOLITUDE

O solitude,
Why are you so
Mesmerizing?

O solitude
Let me immerse
Into your bliss

O solitude
Let me rejoice in your
Sublime beauty

O solitude,
Let me seek myself
In your calm

O solitude,
Let me see the world
In your face

O solitude,
Let me get lost
In your serenity

O solitude,
Let me seek shelter
In your shadow

O solitude,
Let me realize myself
In your quietude

O solitude,
Let me seek my origin
In your permanence

O solitude,
Let me see myself
In your face

O solitude,
Let me dissolve in
Your silence

O solitude,
How shall I fathom
Your depth?

O solitude,
What makes you so serene
And sublime?

O solitude,
Are you the reflection of
My own Self?

O solitude,
Why is your silence
So melodious?

O solitude,
Why are you so full
Of mysteries?

O solitude,
Why are you hiding behind
The veil of silence?

O solitude,
Your flirtation with silence
Is captivating.

O solitude,
What are you hiding
In your void?

O solitude,
Is your void really
Empty or full?

# SCIENCE ASKED

Science asked
Religion: 'Would you
Join my bandwagon?'
Religion replied:
'Sure, if you accept
My doctrine of Self.'
Science remarked:
'No problem, that is what
The cosmos is all about.'

# WORKERS OF THE WORLD ARISE AND AWAKE!

Workers of the world,
Arise and awake!
You don't have to fear anything
But your own submission
Come on, listen to the voice
Of your conscience!

Bring down the walls of prison
Where your conscience is incarcerated
Debunk devious myths woven
In the tenuous thread of equality
Spurn the apocryphal allure
Of establishing your supremacy
Challenge the obsolete monolith
And expose its hideous imposture

O my fellow beings, languishing
In the colossal prisons of Evils,
Arise and awake with all the power
And strength you can ever summon!
Dismantle the demonic order, and
Consign this reeking sin to the
Trash can of human memory

# I WAS LEFT INTRIGUED

As I was once drowned in deep distress,
One day, my Soul suddenly appeared
Before me and said,
"I am really happy with your relentless
Rebellion against untruth, tyranny and injustice."
Even before I could express my sincere
Gratitude, he admired my abiding commitment
To humanity and human beings, too.
I was caught by surprise
When he asked me if I didn't believe in God.
"Of course I do," I replied.
"If so, why are you so distressed?," he enquired.
"I can't see Freedom mutilated, mauled and lynched," I lamented.
Rather brusquely, he asked me if I knew what 'evanescence' was, and
disappeared.
I was left intrigued.

# LIFE IS A HAIKU

Life is a Haiku
Short, yet meaningful
Diminutive, yet profound
Has a clear-cut definition
But never followed
Emphasis laid on Nature
But mostly defied
Just like Haiku
Always flying high
Desperate to cross the limit

# HOW CAN I BELIEVE?

O Creator,
You claim to have created me
But how can I believe in your claim?
Who are you, and what relation do I have with you?
Even if you are true, why did you bestow this mercy upon me?
Have I ever been your benefactor?
Or you want me to be ever-beholden to you?
I always find myself intrigued by your soi disant transcendental existence
Equally am I flummoxed by the esoteric splendor of your immanence
I cannot understand why you are so abstruse and abyssal
Sometimes, I suspect even Narad might have been embroiled in this eternal conundrum
That is what might have turned him into an automated peripatetic human machine
I am wondering if I should contact some monists

# I WANT TO SHARE

O stars, planets and galaxies,
Would you please be my friends?
I want to share my aspirations with you.
Because I know you understand
What a soaring spirit is.
I know you understand
What vastness is,
And you also understand
What immanence is.
How can I exchange my feelings
With those who don't even understand
What greatness really is?

# MY DEAR BARD, I WILL CERTAINLY COME

I will certainly come one day
To your heavenly abode, my dear bard
I have a lot to divulge
About the mortals, and this planet
That have undergone a sea change
Since you left this world one hundred and twenty six years ago
Especially I am impatient to share my feelings and takes
About this great country, we both share
Its people, environment, mountains, plains, prairies,
Rivers, deserts, seas, oceans
Its spectacular scientific and technological advancement
Its momentous achievements in literature, arts, science and philosophy
You might be surprised to know about this great country's perspicacious
leadership
And the way it has redefined freedom and liberty in the light of divinity
within each human Soul
You might be elated to hear about the way it has identified freedom and
democracy as the sole key to achieving human advancement
Certainly you might be mesmerized by the glorious history of American
soldiers
The impeccable legacy of those brave souls that has always served to
rejuvenate the spirit of this great country
America was born out of indomitable spirit of freedom and liberty,
characterizing human Soul
Its creation in itself amounted to the recognition of divinity underlying
each human Soul on earth
O my respected bard, Walt Whitman, I need not launch upon a
harangue on this issue

You know better than me; perhaps you are one among the best who have been successful in recognizing America's transcendental splendor

I feel ecstatic to reminisce the illustrious moments when this great country unswervingly dedicated itself to the cause of freedom and liberty

Its undying commitment to truth and righteousness is also no less inspiring

How America, in spite of formidable odds, prevailed over the forces of untruth and injustice on several occasions are the glowing excerpts of its enviable history

Let's offer our respectful obeisances to the dramatis personae who contributed to the making of this great country's mission a grand success

It makes me grateful, O my respected bard, to recall the seminal role you have played in defining the ultimate mission of this land of the brave

In some respects the 20th century presented itself as the most horrendous episode in human history

Entire humanity was exposed to the most heinous criminality, unleashed by hideous ideologies such as, Nazism, Fascism and communism

Tens of millions of people were forced to succumb to the murderous ambitions of some callous tyrants

And the world was reduced to an unprecedented shambles

I am proud to reveal that under the exceptionally brilliant leadership of our country, a novel international order, based on liberal democracy and free market economy was ushered in

It was not yet immune from diabolic machinations of sinister forces, right until the ignominious demise of the Evil Empire

It did vindicate the primacy of freedom and democracy that we had been consistently emphasizing for the advancement of human society

Most regrettably, a new phenomenon based on eschatological extremism began to haunt our philosophy of freedom and democracy

You might be shocked to hear that these radical Islamic terrorists callously slaughtered three thousand innocent people in simultaneous airline attacks on American soil

But how could this ruthless and heinous crime go unpunished?

They met with a fitting response, resulting in the corrosive disarray of major terrorist group, Al Qaeda, and complete destabilization of Afghanistan that had provided sanctuary for the former

In the wake of our massive military operation, Al Qaida desperately tried to resuscitate itself in the garb of various offshoots, but significantly to no avail

Apparently taking advantage of our temporary vulnerability, arising from nebbishes' indecision and vacillation, a dreaded terrorist organization, named ISIS, raised its hideous face

But its macabre shtick proved short-lived in the face of our determined and unyielding resistance

It gives me immense pleasure and pride to share with you how the seemingly unorthodox voice of lethal strength cowed the North Korean braggadocio into capitulating to our terms on nuclear and ballistic missiles

Much to the chagrin of freedom loving world, China, the home to one and a half billion people, seems sliding towards yet another bout of tyrannical Maoist orthodoxy

No less disappointing is the growing brazenness of Russia, a revanchist force intrinsically bent on checkmating the West, by unleashing repression, murder and espionage, coupled with the annexation of foreign territory

Russia's backing of the Syrian despot seems to have emboldened the murderer of Damascus to use deadly chemical weapons against his own innocent civilians

The malevolent theocracy of Iran, as if further spurred by our episodic policy aberration, is consistently harboring satanic designs, aimed at hammering Western interests

For all the extraordinary performance and sacrifice of our brave servicemen to establish peace and order in Afghanistan, Kabul still seems vulnerable to Taliban's senseless terrorism, presumably aided by the conspiracy of powers that be in Pakistan

Inimical forces - by igniting among the gullible communities lethal impulses, based on race, gender, ethnicity and religion - both within and without, seem intent on getting this country completely torn asunder, so the clarion call for freedom and liberty can be silenced

The ruthless tyranny of Turkey is behaving as if entire world were its sovereignty, thereby exposing its pseudo democratic visage

Despite all this tide against liberal values that we stand for, I am not pessimistic about the future of mankind

Like you, I have full confidence in this country's extraordinary power to salve humanity

As long as America is committed to freedom and liberty of entire mankind, no force on earth can defeat it

Neither can its resplendent aura be diminished by the paroxysmal lightning of some opprobrious tyrants' meteoric rise

O Greatest poet of America, I feel exulted to share with you that our scientific adventure has touched a new high; we are effectively on the way of turning humans into multi-planetary species

Hollywood, however facing some hitches, stemming from jaundiced and malicious agendas - quite inconsistent with its existential rationale - has retained its position, as the torchbearer of our ever expanding socio-cultural influence

O my dear bard, I have taken it as a privilege and honor to have an opportunity to share all these things with you

I know you are as much proud of this country of freedom and liberty as I am

I know you are as much fascinated with the brave people of this country as I am

I know you are as much smitten with the glorious history and natural beauty of this country as I am

Virtually inspired by you I, too, sing myself

I sing myself in every creature on earth

I sing myself in everything that moves in this universe

I sing myself in everything that is stagnant in this universe

I sing myself in the infinity, eternity and imperishability of the power behind this cosmos

I sing myself in the ubiquity, immanence and equipoise of the power behind the creation, sustenance and dissolution

Above everything else, I sing myself in the beauty, fragrance and music of creation

We will keep celebrating them ad infinitum since we both realize that we are none other than them

We are the hub unto which meet infinite spokes of creation

# LET ME REVEL

O my Soul,
Let me keep eulogizing you as long as I am alive
You are in the earth, you are in water, you are in fire,
you are in space and you are in air
There is nothing in this cosmos where I can't find you
Each and everything, from tiny atom to the cosmos, owes its existence
to your mercy
Were it not for your will how could this cosmos have come into
existence?
I know, the day will come when you will choose to annihilate it en
masse, only to create a new one
Really, how exhilarating your transcendental pastime is; and how
mysterious your modus operandi!
Pray let me revel in your mesmerizing *Lila* till eternity

# SOMETIMES I INHALE POIGNANCY

Sometimes I inhale poignancy and exhale poems
This is how I write my destiny on the pages of Time
I am a bard never born before in the annals of humans
With me, I always carry on my shoulder the fate of humanity
I am an eternal witness to the evolution of this cosmos
Before my eyes it will one day shrink into an infinitesimal dot
Poets are mostly seen to have dwelt on amatory gossips and amorous
fantasies
But I don't want to waste my time on such impish trifles
I want to ignite massive conflagration inside each human
So he might burn entire complacency and inertia to ashes, and rise with
the true spirit of his Soul
I want to see each human completely free and liberated

# BUSY, BUSY, BUSY

Busy, busy, busy
So busy, always busy
So much so that
I am afraid
Maybe I won't have time
Even to die

# ATROCITY OF TIME

I am but a mute statue of composite elements
Each passing moment measures my mortal existence
It is beyond my capacity to destroy even a fraction of that moment
Time, however subtle and impalpable, is the greatest totalitarian dictator
Under its overarching command, I always get crushed into smithereens
My protests and remonstrations have turned out to be an eternal cry in
wilderness
Having been enslaved since time immemorial, I seem to have lost my
conscience
I have been a dry leaf woefully abandoned by the tree
Even a slight provocation of wind makes me waft aimlessly in the air
I am not sure, how many cycles of creation ought to be completed before
I embark on my own conscience,
And retaliate against the atrocity of Time

# CATS CATCH MICE

Cats catch mice, they cherish blood
Blood is their religion, blood their creed
Mice are submissive, yet mischievous
Doctrinaire they are, they have their own philosophy – pusillanimity

Cats and mice
Mice and cats
Blood and philosophy
Philosophy and blood

Struggle between cats and mice, highly skewed balance of power
Missiles and mortars, bombs and rockets determine the trajectory of
human destiny
When mutilated bodies and maimed souls define the order of the day
humanity groans in excruciating agony
Hitler's oratory devours Buddha's compassion, and neurotic asteroids
blow up Yin Yang into pieces

It is not possible for mice to survive cats' onslaught
They are killed,
They are murdered
They are assassinated

Cats cherish blood
Blood is their philosophy,
Blood their creed

# WITH A COURTESAN

You cannot seduce me
Because, to me,
You are nothing but a statue
Your eyes are hollow
They are dreadful black holes
Your nose, an ugly protuberance
Your lips, snares of passion
Your breasts, dreadful massifs,
Exuding intoxicating attachment
Your navel, a whirlpool,
Leading to the nadir of lust
Your hands, walls of the eternal prison
Your legs, a movement toward
Mesmerizing netherworld
Where orgy is confused with samadhi
Your hair, fierce darkness,
Befalling my destiny
Curvature of your body,
Byzantine alley,
Fraught with ravenous ghosts
Your smile, poison coated with nectar
Your amorous advance,
Prognosis of my destruction
Still, I salute the Soul,
Lurking behind your corporeal existence
Because that is none
Other than my own Self

# I DON'T WANT TO CRY

It so occurs to me sometimes, as if
I don't want to cry, I don't want to weep
I can't smile and laugh, either
I have turned into the autumn, steadily shedding its own existence
My mind is ossified, and my heart frozen
My conscience is paralyzed, and my Soul incarcerated
I feel like I have been sucked into the harrowing whirlpool of my own life
In spite of myself, I seem hurtling towards the bottommost depth of the ocean
O lord, why don't you disconnect me from myself before I hit the nadir
of my own destiny

# FORCED TO DISSOLVE

These days I can't write anything
My hands are paralyzed
My head is empty

Rivers have ceased to flow
The wind is loath to blow
Flowers are reluctant to bloom
The world has turned into the gloom

I cannot reminisce my beginning
Neither can I fathom my end
I have always remained a void
Devoid of shape and size
Length and breadth
Height and depth

I don't manifest in my own shadows
They are sovereign and independent
My ego cannot ruffle their silence
They are defiantly mute

I am forced to dissolve
Into the Stygian darkness
Of their eternal scorn

# ENEMY HAS YET TO BE IDENTIFIED

Every moment is rife with tension
New frontiers are created
Fault lines are already defined
Rockets and mortars, artilleries and grenades, aircraft carriers and
bombs are amassed
But still, the war is not likely to break out,
Because the enemy has yet to be identified

# ENJOYING ILLUSION

Humans have a tendency of enjoying illusion
They are apprehensive of truth and reality
Truth, to them, is naked and reality obscene
It takes enormous moxie to acknowledge truth
Reality renders one lurid and exposed
Untruth and illusion are invariably cherished

# I WAS DISSOLVING

One day I felt like I was steadily dissolving
I was stunned, I was scarred, and I began to cry
Since I was in extreme trauma, I prayed to God
The ground beneath my feet was sinking
The sky above my head was falling
I was frantic in search of help
I wished some Messiah came and rescued me from being devastated
I cried and cried and cried, but to no avail
Entire ambience was mum, even the cosmos was observing silence, as if
to further frighten me
Completely helpless, I felt cruelly cornered by my destiny
With all options exhausted, I rose in revolt with all the strength I could muster
Violently I recoiled
All of a sudden, I found myself fallen off my cot,
And I came to my senses
It was nothing but a dream

# I WANT TO FORGET

I want to forget myself in poems
They are the vibrations of my being, effervescent and incandescent
They provide color to my emotions
My life, a fleeting meteorite, is an evanescent spasm of art
To me, both life and death are unforgettable milestones of a poetic
journey

# IF I EVER DREAM OF ...

If I ever dream of ...
Forgive me

Your lips are roses
Exuding eternal fragrance

Your eyes,
Wonderful receptacle
Of hypnotic exuberance

As if to survive
The inflictions of destiny,
I feel like hiding
Into the clouds of your black hair

My eyes get inebriated
Even at the sight of your curve

Intoxication of your furtive glances
Renders me oblivious
To my own existence

If I ever dream of ...
Forgive me

# LOVE

Love is transparent; it is vivacious
Valor and chivalry add to its magnificence
It is oblivious to the dynamics of time and space
It is an emotional projectile that aims at hitting the naught

# POEM OF NATURE

Man is the poem written by Nature
With the indelible ink of spirit
He is an idyllic landscape of emotions
Through which Nature expresses itself
God speaks through his heart, and
Time seeks its future in his toil
On his wisdom lies the vast space,
The foundation of the universe
Man is his own destination,
There is nothing beyond him

# MILK

Smoke does not come out of a glass of milk
Once boiled, it speaks through its vapor, hot and moisturizing
Although it is white, it does not deliver harangues on peace, harmony
and coexistence
It can upset your stomach if you are lacto-sensitive
To some, it's got numinous import; it is a panacea to numerous diseases
My grandma used to say: It works wonder when you are neurasthenic
But I am not sure
I am sure about one thing - it provides nourishment to both Devils and
Gods alike

# WE ARE MUMMIES

We are
Mummies,
Hidden in
Pyramids of
Egypt

Hideous
And
Erosive,
Yet
Invaluable

A link
Between
Two worlds,
Tow times,
Two spaces

Dead
Still alive,
Silent
Still voluble,
Ugly
Still beautiful

A mystery,
With impeccable
Attraction

# I HAD HAD A DREAM

Last night I had had a dream
It was a white one - fluid, shapeless and highly concentrated
It also seemed tight, enlarged, and considerably elongated
My dream splashed all over your soaring lust and passions
I could not see you, neither could I feel your existence
When my dream hit its climax I was entirely sucked into a black hole
With my physical existence reduced to almost zero
I was all consciousness - transcendental and unimaginably ecstatic
My dream finally turned into a void - inscrutable, yet resounding with euphoria
Presumably a divine prelude to the beginning of a new world
It was really a wonderful dream

# SUN IN SEARCH OF A NEW BRIDE

Sun is perhaps in search of a new bride
He is not satisfied with Moon
To him, Moon is no longer sensuous and beautiful
She seems tired, bedraggled and disheveled
She has also become too cold
Apparently, mortified at her reduced libido,
She is trying to hide herself behind the clouds
The fear of potential estrangement
Has added to her agony and torture
She always cries in solitude
There is but none to console her
Save the caressing of loneliness
Every morning we see her tears
Collected by plants with empathy
But that, too, Sun cannot tolerate

# STILL A NIGHTMARE

Old age,
Sickness
And death

Siddhartha's
Passion
For eternity

Detachment
From worldly
Pleasures

Self-mortification -
A torturous
Journey

Realization
Of the
Absolute

The world
Still a
Nightmare

# BUT THERE WAS NO RESPONSE

Reproached and reproved
By my own family,
I knocked on the doors of temples
But there was no response

Snubbed and stigmatized
By my own neighbors,
I knocked on the doors of churches
But there was no response

Humiliated and hated
By my own relatives,
I knocked on the doors of mosques
But there was no response

Despised and disparaged
By my own society,
I knocked on the doors of synagogues
But there was no response

Persecuted and punished
By state authorities,
I knocked on the doors of monasteries
But there was no response

O lord, every time I came to you
In fervent anticipation of your love,
Mercy and compassion,
I found myself spurned

Virtually,
I was left with no choice
But to turn to my own Being
That eventually bestowed
Ineffable solace upon me
Verily, you were nowhere
Save in my own Soul

# PERHAPS MY LIFE IS NOT HAPPY WITH ME

Since long I have been trying to write a poem on my life
Despite frantic efforts it does not occur to me what to write
When I try to project my life as something fluid, it turns out to be solid
When I try to describe its solidity it morphs into something fluid
The moment I give in to its eccentricity and acknowledge its both
fluidity and solidness, it starts evaporating
I have no idea why it is trying to play truant with me
The more I want to hold on to it the more I find it estranged
Perhaps my life is not happy with me
Maybe, like an embarrassed and annoyed tenant, it is trying to find a
new apartment

# NOWHERE COULD YOU BE SEEN

I rummaged in
The entire holy Scriptures,
But nowhere could You be seen

I was really exulted
When I saw You smiling at me
Once I peered
Into the afflicted hearts
Of my own fellow beings

# MAY I HAVE YOUR PERMISSION?

My love,
May I have your permission
To fathom the oceans of your eyes?

My love,
May I have your permission
To drink the nectar of your lips?

My love,
May I have your permission
To scale the mountain of your breasts?

My love,
May I have your permission
To explore the black hole of your universe?

My love,
May I have your permission
To reside in a corner of your heart?

# MUSINGS

Each individual, in one way or another, contributes to the harmony and coherence of Nature.

---

Nature does not make any distinction between the opposites. It is transcendental to the dynamics of emotions and impulses.

---

At his core each human is a Singularity where science ends and speculation begins.

---

Since Philosophy has a symbiotic relationship with the basic character of human Soul, there is no question of its dying, no matter how profoundly it gets buffeted by the momentous strides of Science.

---

The dazzling beauty, radiating from entire paraphernalia of Nature, is nothing but the solemn reflection of our own Soul whose divine spell has wrapped the universe, both from within and without.

---

I have always found the conversation between Solitude and Man replete with the echo of some sublime message that human societies tend to reverberate with.

---

The mute vastness of the universe can be likened to the celestial silence of our conscience that is the mainstay of entire forces, responsible for creating, sustaining and dissolving the cosmos.

---

Apparently swayed by the impetuous wind, my senses sometimes tend to embark on amorous escapades, with complete disregard for what my conscience fondly cherishes.

---

No matter whether it is a word or a sentence, it represents the lifeline of my existence that is nothing but the sense of being, reverberating in my mind, word and deed.

---

We are but the imprint of tears and smiles, ensuing from our contact with multitudinous dimensions of creation in the core of which lies the existence of our Being.

---

Even the black clouds hovering over our destiny cannot presage our extinction provided that we are committed to shoring up our shared values, irrespective of our disparate identities.

---

Diving deep into my own Being, I am always trying to explore the innumerable mysteries of cosmos, in which is hidden the secret history of our existence.

# MOST BEAUTIFUL POEM

I am the most beautiful poem
I am beyond entire constraints
I can't be confined to any limitations
Nor can I be defined by prejudiced minds
Even the stereotype of time and space
Cannot influence my ethereal existence
Sometimes, I manifest myself
In the majestic loftiness of mountains, and
At other times, in the tranquil depth of oceans
In the realm of my imagination
There is no difference between
Flowers and thorns,
Ecstasy and agony,
I am equipoised and steadfast
I believe in creation
I pursue the rhythm and rhyme of both life and death
Infinity in style and content
Adds substance to my Being
I am neither beautiful nor ugly
Neither mellifluous nor cacophonous
I am how I am perceived
I am what I am,
Indeed,
Beyond the compass of
Mortals' comprehension

# I AM POLITY

You smile
I ignore

You laugh
I dismiss

You speak
I pout

You cry
I scorn

You writhe
I rejoice

You fall
I push

You stand
I shove

Want to know
My identity?

I am
Polity

# I WANT TO SPREAD

However a Lilliputian entity, my shadow threatens me with hideous deformations and distortions
I find the geography of my Being constricted under the intimidating sky of my own shadow
It prevents the syllables of my existence from getting printed on the pages of time
I don't want to be miniaturized; I don't want to be relegated to a microscopic dot
I want to spread across the vast universe

# A FLEETING METEORITE

Those who fail to respond to Time's injunctions will find themselves brushed aside

Time is not only a movement, it is a revolution, with the potential of turning the entire universe upside down

The wrath of Time has burnt many a mighty empire to ashes

Completely indifferent to human emotions, Time can morph itself into a dreadful monster

Atavistically protean, Time can also sometimes turn itself into a fleeting meteorite of one's destiny

# WE ARE FOREVER

The world
We live in
Looks so beautiful

It is gorgeous
Its splendors abound
It is unbelievably idyllic

Days smile
At the blooming of flowers, and
The flowing of rivers

Twinkling of stars, and
Shining of the Moon
Add to the beauty of night

Silence of solitude
Whispers the melody of love
Life becomes ecstatic

My Love
You need not worry
Even if I depart

Everywhere
You will find me,
From fragrance of flowers
To the frolicking of streams

Just close your eyes
For a moment, and seek
You will find me within yourself

I am no different from you
Nor are you different from me
We are but one

Once we are
We are forever
Never shall vanish
Our Soul, my Dear

# A YOGI TIRED OF LIFE

A yogi
Tired
Of life

Doesn't
Want to
Die

Neither
Commits
Suicide

Gives a
New definition
To life

Nirvana and Moksha
Both
Pursue him

# A DREAM, HORRID AND SURREAL

Recently I had had a very strange dream -
Surreal, telltale, horrifying and ominous.

In a desolate plateau, surrounded by naked
mountains, visibly streaked by exhausted brooks,
Lord Krishna was being crucified.

Evidently overpowered by muscular buffoons,
He was being nailed unto a big Cross.

With His head lowered, more by civilizational decay
than by the physical torture meted out to him,
He was sheepishly following the brutal command
of scapegraces, fanatically aligned with corrupt, puritanical and
kleptomaniac priesthood.

Witnessed was this horrid ordeal by a circumference of so-called movers
and shakers of the contemporary world, including his own relations.

Strangely enough,
this episode was immediately succeeded by
a rather astounding event, seemingly exhilarating,
yet prognostic, and probably pregnant with dire imponderables.

Attired in traditional robes, radiating the majesty and grandeur of
Hindu deities,
Jesus was seen dancing with thousands of gopikas.

Even amidst the cacophonous din of inscrutable chanting,
Jesus could easily be seen deeply immersed in amorous revelry.

Visibly insensitive to the expectations and aspirations of mortals,
He seemed to have consigned himself to the lustful realm of sensual
ecstasy.

Not surprisingly, there stood a phalanx of distinguished clergy
to vicariously savor their master's *raasleela*.

What was still dumbfounding was that it was not the end of my dream.

The third episode is no less captivating,
yet intimidating, portentous and, potentially cataclysmic.

I saw Muhammad resurrecting from his tomb.

With Koran in his right hand and *Sudarshan Chakra* in his left,
He was roaring, as if He was bent on settling score with humanity itself,
apparently for its having hobnobbed with *kafirs*.

Thousands of imams and mullahs, attired in pitch black,
were seen singing his praise.

The ambience appeared shuddering with the call of the muezzin,
presumably hurtling from the distant past.

In the aftermath of these three episodes in quick succession,
my Conscience - who stood before me in person – asked me,
"As an ordinary citizen of this world, given to tolerance and respect
for all religions and faiths, what do you make of this rather bizarre
panoramic view of the divine authorities?"

It was not so much his sensitivity towards my sentiments that stroke
chord with me. Rather, it was his deep concern for human beings and
humanity that have always thrived in the sublime shadows of those
highly respected saviors.

But having been completely benumbed by what I had seen with my own eyes, I could not utter even a word.

Perhaps my words would not have been so much eloquent as my anguished silence had been.
And it could hardly escape the prescient discernment of my Conscience.

"Don't worry," With deep empathy towards my tortured emotions and traumatized impulses, my Conscience, in a solemn voice, said, '*Naasato vidyate bhaavo naabhaavo vidyate satah*'.

Suddenly, I found myself violently yanked by the deafening thunderbolt, preceded by the rather sardonic smile of piercing lightning. Thus I awoke to a completely different world - enslaved, tyrannized and plaintive.

It was the night of summer. Saturnine sky was pouring overwhelmingly. Probably agonized at potential forebodings, the earth was hiding herself in the dark.

Poor humans! How could they read what was written on the wall of their destiny? Benighted and nescient, they seemed snuggling up with the beguiling joy of sleep.

I found myself torn between the dread of dream and the comfort – however evanescent – of the real world. But to me, there was still something common between the two realms: deep apprehension about the future of humanity.

# HOW CAN I CONCEAL MYSELF?

From the bottommost
Corner of my heart,
Silence one day was overheard murmuring:
"If you accept my reign, you will enjoy eternal peace."
My conscience responded, "But how can I conceal myself in a deep
recess like you?"

# IN SEARCH OF A QUESTION

For many years
I am in search of a question
That I want to ask my destiny
But my failure to find the one
Has prodded my destiny to sneer at me,
"Isn't your life a question in itself?"

# WHERE THERE IS DARK, THERE IS LIGHT

There comes a certain moment
In your life, when you get
Completely benighted
You can't even think
Who you are
Perhaps this is the point of time
Wherefrom starts the process
Of your being enlightened
Because where there is dark
There is light

# I AM SMITTEN WITH YOU

Having been immersed
In the solitude
Of my own Being,
One day I asked life,
"Why do you pursue me?"
With a serene streak of smile
In his glowing face,
He replied:
"Because I am smitten with you."

# HAVE YOU EVER SEEN?

Have you ever seen Sun
Turn into an icy stone?
Have you ever seen
That celestial body
Metamorphose into a tiny ball?
It does, it really does change itself
Many a time I have seen it
Even cave in to celestial amour
When its passions start boiling
It strives to pour itself out
Looks for some tender corner
In the Milky Way galaxy
And enjoys cathartic ecstasy

# AN ETERNAL ENIGMA

Whence starts the inquiry into the nature of reality?
Whence starts the pursuit of life, liberty and happiness?
Whence starts the search for fellowship among human beings?
Whence starts the quest for truth, underlying the phenomenal world?
Whence starts the exploration of the abyssal cosmos?
Whence starts the eternal journey of the unknown?
O my Soul,
You are not only the sole answer
But also the sole cause, source and inspiration
An eternal enigma, rooted in our own divinity

# I PREACH REVOLUTION

I believe in Revolution
Therefore, I call myself a Revolutionary

I am always in favor of a cataclysmic change
Yes, I agree with Nietzsche:
God is already dead

I don't have trust in any belief systems
I have a strong aversion to religion
I am an atheist

Philosophy, for me, wields mere meretricious charm
I don't believe in caste, creed, sex and sect
Temples and monasteries, for me, are
Vestiges of arrogance
Mosques and churches archaic anachronism

Buddha, for me, is a meek nincompoop
Jesus a daredevil
Krishna a playboy, and
Mohammad a fanatical extremist

I don't believe in freedom,
Because it is nothing but a lollipop
I don't believe in sovereignty;
It is a deceptive rhetoric

Democracy, it is really an ogre
I don't want it to ogle at me
What are human rights?
Nothing, but a timid passion for condescension

I don't love my country;
It teaches me chauvinism and parochialism
I want to see the total elimination of all institutions:
Marriage, family, convention and tradition
Nor have I any attachment to relations

I hate compassion
I detest fraternity and brotherhood
I abhor freedom and equality
I have a mordant contempt for love and affection
Amity, cordiality and amiability are nothing
But poison that destroys my nerves

Friends are my immediate enemies
I harbor hostility towards neighbors

Blood is my nectar,
Violence my creed,
And destruction my culling

Sabotage is my philosophy,
Terrorism my principle,
And anarchy my ideal

I am the absolute reality
I am the absolute truth
I am beyond the touch of time and space
There is nothing that can destroy me

I am the supreme
I am omniscient
I am omnipresent
I am omnipotent

The voice within me incessantly howls:
Lead me from truth to untruth
From light to darkness, and
From immortality to death

Untruth, darkness and death represent solemnity for me
Unlike Buddha and other countless seers,
I realize both Moksha and Nirvana through them

Buddha, from his deathbed, said to Anand:
"Be ye lamp unto yourself,
Hold fast to the truth as a lamp"

Sermons! That too from a melancholic derelict?
What can be more ludicrous than this?
Perhaps, Gautam would have come to senses
Had he followed at least in the footsteps of Charvaka

However, it is my passionate plea:
That the Buddhas, seers and sages to come
Devoutly pursue my path
Let them have courage even to spurn the cowherd, who exhorted:
*"Sarbadharman parityajya mamekam sharanam braja"*

Because I am a Revolutionary
I preach Revolution

January 25, 2004

(This poem is a satire on Maoists and their so-called People's War that,
in a decade beginning 1996, cost the lives of more than 16 thousand
Nepalese, and destroyed Nepal's infrastructure on a massive scale)

# PATH TO THE UNKNOWN

The path
To the unknown
Is strewn with
Innumerable corpses
Of venerable martyrs
Who
Sacrificed their
Precious lives
In search of Truth
That inspires humanity
To preserve its sanctity
Through the cultivation
Of love and compassion
In every heart

# HOW DARE YOU TRAMPLE?

O tyrants of the world,
How dare you trample
On our fate?

Try not to muzzle our voice
It might turn into thunderbolts

Try not to extinguish our conscience
It might turn into lethal nukes

Try not to inhume our existence
It might reduce you to ashes

Don't ever try to toy
With humanity;
It has already resurrected

# EVERY MOMENT IS A CHALLENGE

Every moment is a challenge
A challenge of biblical proportion
Either light or dark; either life or death
We have to make the choice ourselves

Our existence depends upon how adaptive we can be to the eccentric
fluidity of Time
Time can be both: compassionate and devastative
Slight inadvertence on our part can turn Time into an implacable foe

Even an extremely subtle and diaphanous veil of Time wields the
potential of causing cosmic upheavals
Time's judgmental authority has never been questioned
Even the destiny of the Almighty can be changed by the decree of Time
Time's infallibility has ubiquitously been accepted

# ILLUSION

There was no past
There is no present
There will be no future
There is no life
There is no death
There is neither time nor space
Everything visible is an illusion
Everything invisible is an illusion
We ourselves are an illusion
Illusion itself is an illusion

# JOURNEY OF MY LIFE

I have found myself dissolved
In the intoxication of your beauty
I have found my amorous senses
Reinvigorated by your furtive glances
I have found the fragrance of spring
Exuding from your enigmatic smiles
I have found myself exalted
By the ecstasy of your presence
To me, you are the embodiment of
*Satyam, Shivam and Sundaram*
I am not sure about the destination, but
The journey of my life begins from you

# NATURE'S CONGRUENCE

The sun is
Scorching and
The moon placid

The sky is
Overarching and
The ocean insatiate

The wind is
Impetuous and
The mountain arrogant

The stream is
Cacophonous and
The river defiant

Where shall I
Find the congruence
Of Nature?

# LIFE IS AN ENIGMA

No pleasure
No pain - but still,
Life is vivid

No smile
No tears - but still,
Life is intoxicating

No victory
No defeat - but still,
Life is enchanting

No profit
No loss - but still,
Life is fascinating

No love
No hate - but still,
Life is alluring

Sure,
Life is an enigma
That never unfolds

# LOOK AT YOURSELF

If you look at yourself you will find your nerves entangled in the arithmetic of your senses

You will find your freedom incarcerated in the cobweb of desire and ambition

Your peace of mind has been a hostage to deceptive optimism and devious hopes

You are nothing but an inanimate statue of God who can neither smile nor cry

Your destiny has confined you to a small temple - dilapidated and ramshackle

You are destined to view the world in silent agony that never ends

# INEXPLICABLE ENIGMA

We seem tiny worms and insects
With infinitesimal existence,
Often prone to extinction
Vibration of our conscience
Can hardly shake the universe
We die the instant we are born
Distance between our life and death
Defines the geography of our being
Still, we are an inexplicable enigma,
Potential enough to create the cosmos

# I FEEL LIKE DRINKING THE MOON

I feel like drinking the moon
And munching on the sun
Even the entire oceans of earth
Cannot quench my thirst
Stars, the golden popcorns,
Are too light to satisfy my hunger
I am no longer a tiny human
Whining in front of idols and deities
Now, I have realized my true Being
I can gorge on millions of galaxies
Without any complaints of indigestion
I am the cosmic ubermensch
Corporeal Fuhrers are my valets
Who tie the lace of my shoes
Every morning, before I set out
For extra-terrestrial escapades
Rambha, Tilottama and Urbashi
Are too few to extinguish the
Conflagration of my libido
It is only because of the perennial light
Of my *jyotirlinga* that the cosmos
Finds itself illumined and incandescent

# AND TIME PROSTRATES

Time speaks the stillness of solitude
It listens to nobody's prayer
It is ruthless, callous and condescending
Even the high-pitched shrilling of cicada
Cannot make it veer off its course
It is poised, composed and unfazed
In the endless realm of Time
We are infinitesimal beings -
Some among us can be classified as
Insidious microbes and viruses
Often in search of pliant preys
Nero's brain is a microcosm of Time
A deep cauldron in which are blended
Sadomasochism and psychedelic fantasies
Blood of the innocent is the red vermilion
Propitiating the forehead of Time
Unlike us, Hitler and Mussolini,
Stalin and Mao were not humans
They were the evil paws of Time
Indeed, Time sometimes reincarnates itself
As the brutal custodian of gulags,
Concentration camps and gas chambers
When Time meets with an accident
People like Lincoln and Gandhi are born
And Time prostrates before them in expiation

# THE WORLD ITSELF HAS TURNED EROTIC

Tears of Yashohdhara
Could not deter Siddhartha
From pursuing
The path of the unknown
Neither could Xanthippe's petulance
Stop Socrates from
Embarking on gnothi seauton
Buddha was a prelude to Socrates, and
Socrates was the Buddha reborn
Trailblazers of human civilization,
Both have been turned into mercantile
Objects and sold at boutique centers
They seem pale when compared
With the splendor of erotic icons
True, the world itself has turned erotic
Buddha and Socrates are not supposed
To impart orgiastic pleasure

# I HAD DIED A THOUSAND TIMES

When I was assailed
By the harrowing moments of
Despondence, I desperately tried
To find you

I rummaged through the
Pages of my heart
I dived into the depth
Of my sight

But alas!
I could not find you anywhere
You were neither hidden in my soul
Nor were you immersed into my being

I found myself deserted
Even by your shadow
It was the moment of my utmost sadness
When I had died a thousand times

# HOW ASTONISHING!

How astonishing!
The world is nothing
But *maya*, an illusion
Nothing is real!
Everything a mirage
Deceptive reflection of Time and Space
Exceptionally wondrous magical feat
Just a sleight of hand!
But who is it that performs this miracle?

# THUS REVEAL THEMSELVES

Ricocheting off the sanctum of dark
Divine vibration hits the Super Soul
Whose existence finds itself expressed in Big Bang,
Followed by the cosmic sound of Om
Thus reveal themselves the mystery of His creation,
The majesty and grandeur of His divine persona, and
The ultimate Law of Nature

# AMERICA, YOU MUST BE STUNNED

O America,
You must have been stunned again at the callousness of the murderous regime of Bashar Assad
Look, how innocent little angels are excruciatingly gasping for a morsel of air
How could the Demon of Damascus subject dozens of children and women to such ruthless agony?
How dared he use lethal chlorine gas against his own people, only to perpetuate a hellish nightmare?
America, you must be equally shocked at the conscious complicity of Russia and Iran in Assad's macabre pursuit
Once again Douma has reminded the entire world of the horrendous saga of Hitler's atrocities
Devilish ambitions of irredentist Russia and apocalyptic Iran have further emboldened the barbarous Assad regime to revel in the agony and torture of innocent Syrians
Much to the indignation of entire world, Russia seems morphed into a horrific monster with growing crave for blood and territory
Even Tolstoy in his grave might be convulsing at the Russian leadership's dastardly complicity in the gruesome killing of Syrian children and women
America, how can you be a passive spectator to the way this Axis of Evil - comprising Syria, Russia and Iran - is trying to strangulate the norms and practices of a civilized world?
No nation on earth should be allowed to launch such a savage attack on humanity with impunity
America, it is natural for the whole world to expect a fitting response from you, with a view to teaching a timely lesson to recidivist perpetrators

April 10, 2018

# YOU ARE THE ONE TO DEFINE THE ORDER

O my Soul,
You have pervaded not only America
You have embraced the whole world
You hanker after democracy, the heartbeat of humanity
You insist on rule of law, the magic key to order
You persist in justice, the jewel of civilization
You seek equality, as a recognition of divinity in each individual
You cry for freedom, the ultimate destination of mankind
You are the one to define the order not only in human societies
But also in distant worlds of celestial bodies

# PROFOUND FAITH IN MYSELF

I possess tremendous hope
about my life and my future

The source of my hope is not
my belief in any imaginary God

Rather it is a profound faith in my Self
as the only source of divinity and godliness

I believe,
I am not an inanimate admixture
of blood, bones and flesh,

A trifle, amenable to
the hideous horrors of mortal world,

A pipsqueak. easily frightened
by the minatory thunders
of extra-terrestrial forces

I am an integral part
of the indestructible power,
that sustains the cosmos

Even the life of cosmos
is attributed to my eternity

Verily,
*Aham Brahmashmi!*

# I HAVE NO QUALMS

O lord, I have no qualms
for what I have been destined to.

Devoid of compunction I am
for the trifle I have been reduced to.

You gave me life, you gave me color;
I sing your love, I sing your power.

# I DON'T KNOW

I don't know
why
something always
struggles to explode
from within me,
only to render
this world
bright, luminous
and enlightened.

# NAUGHT BE THY DESTINY

Behind the shadow
of my imaginations,
I find reincarnation and moksha
constantly writhing in agony.

Just like fish,
stripped of their natural abode,
I find them asphyxiated
and struggling for life.

I do understand their trauma;
I do recognize their terminal throes.
But I am completely helpless.

We are separated
by an unfathomable abyss
heavily infested by
arrogance, hubris and ignorance.

Narked at being ignored mercilessly,
they mutter imprecation on me:
'Naught be thy destiny'

# TRY NOT TO INCARCERATE

Let me see,
let me taste,
let me smell,
let me touch,
let me listen.

Try not
to incarcerate
my senses.

They represent the first
line of defense
when it comes to my
freedom and liberty.

# MORPHED INTO A NYMPH

Once I saw
the most expensive car
on the internet.

I found it sleek, slender and trendy.
Just like the nymph of my imagination,
it was really scintillating, and titillating.

The more I got my eyes fixated on it
the more I found my senses
desperate to savor the beauty of a nymph.

As if in deference to my urge
the car suddenly morphed into a nymph.
I don't think it was mere a coincidence.

# I WANT TO SPEND

Life is too short to be expended in the quest for long and languorous
sentences
I want to spend my whole life in search of a single word that can best
explore the eternal fate of mankind,
As well as the endless mysteries,
Lurking behind the cosmic phenomena
Because I know, word is Brahma -
The divine origin of both cause and effect,
And the beginning and end

# HOW LONG?

O my destiny,
How long do I need to loiter in your condescension
Before I can identify my destination -
Probably an idyllic rendezvous
Where the beginning and end of creation commiserate
In a spirit of inexorable interchangeability
Between science and spirituality

# CADAVEROUS FACE

Cadaverous face
of the Earth
constantly torments me

Mute, helpless and quivering,
she looks to me
with plaintive eyes

A sickly soul,
wrecked by its own body

What can I do
to redress her agony?

# WHILE READING BOOKS

While reading books,
I sometimes find myself
in the labyrinthine alleys
of someone's erudition
where my sense of direction
woefully disappears

# AN ELUSIVE DESTINATION

Evanescence
of snow flakes
juxtaposed with
immortality of love

Oceans of my tears
passionately cherish
an amorous embrace of moon

Sphinx,
smoldering in eternal agony,
seeks refuge
in the silence of its own Being

Love,
An elusive destination --
intoxicating seduction
of a femme fatale

# HE WAS NOWHERE

With existence
steadily maimed and mutilated
by endless violence and terror,
humanity tried to seek refuge
in the Almighty
But alas! He was nowhere
to respond to its plaintive groaning
It was unimaginably shocked
when it suddenly found Him
commiserating with the lunatic
bigotry of pandas, clerics and mullahs.

# MACBETHS OF THE WORLD, BEWARE!

Macbeth is seized with horror
His hands are stained with blood
Since Macbeth has murdered the sleep itself,
He can sleep no more

Demonic ambition
Landed him in the realm of
Infinite torture and agony

What really led Macbeth and his wife
To complete destruction; his own
Ambition or the witches' prophesies?

Was it mere a coincidence
Or a diktat of the nemesis?
Macbeths of the world, beware!
Ambition will lead you nowhere

Engrave your heart with this lesson
Or else you'll end up in devastation

# BUT HIS PLAYTHINGS

Civilization is the face of man,
Culture his behavior, and
Religion temperament
Man creates his own sun
He creates his own moon
Stars and oceans,
Mountains and deserts
Are nothing,
But his playthings,
Trivial and evanescent

# A TRUTH, PURE AND UNVARNISHED

Birds sing
Flowers bloom
Rivers flow
Stars twinkle
Is there any common thread that binds them together?
Is there any relation between our consciousness and innumerable objects
that bedeck this universe?
How are we related to the multiverse?
Krishna and the Buddha are not the answers
They are just enchanting phenomena, raising more questions than
answers
Neither the principle of Karma nor the esoteric philosophy of Nirvana
can provide absolute solution to the ailment of malfunctioning
consciousness
A cosmic problem demands a cosmic solution
In reality, the mystery of the cosmos lies in the divine innocence of a
child
He has always remained a pioneer in the exploration of human
consciousness
Celestial ecstasy exudes from his smile
A pristine source of energy, capable of reinvigorating the order of human
consciousness
Child is the messiah
Reverential deity of the earth
A truth,
Pure and unvarnished

# WE DON'T BELIEVE

We are the shadows of grave
We go where the graves are
We are keen to be dissolved into soil
We are soil, we are water
We are fire, we are air
We are in the space
And space is within us
We are subject to continuous cycle of implosion and explosion
Empires wax and wane
Emperors become naked
But nobody dares reveal
It is a small child that says: The emperor is naked
Truth is explosive
It is pregnant with millions of tons of weapons grade plutonium
It can wreak havoc and turn our universe upside down
The veracity of the Buddha's enlightenment and the Christ's resurrection
has always remained shrouded in eternal mystery
Humans are not prepared to be overwhelmed by the mushroom cloud
We don't believe it has any silver lining

# TIME WOULD HAVE MOURNED

In the sweltering heat of July
An old man sits under a huge peepul tree, savoring the sacred shade
Starts contemplating the life hereafter
Nostalgic about the vibrant youth, idyllic romance and luxuriant,
amatory escapades
Heaves a sigh of wistfulness
Religion, spirituality, altruism and renunciation all appear to be the
groaning of a deer, haunted by ferocious tiger
*Mahabhinishkramana* of the Buddha sounds hollow and vacuous to him
Peers into the vast sky, constantly burning with the ire of Sun
Suddenly the image of Sun God, driving his divine chariot, comes to his
mind
Almost mechanically bows his head in obeisance
Deep yearning, oscillating between temporal pleasure and liberation
from the cycle of birth and death, leaves him eternally obfuscated
Were the pendulum enlightened, Time would have certainly mourned
its loss

# WHY DID YOU MAKE US?

How can a life,
based on tenuous relationship
between the light and dark,
produce eternal ecstasy?
O God,
if you have chosen
not to give permanence to our life,
why did you make us
so much attached to it?

# WE FEAR EVERYTHING RELATING TO DEATH

The dead are more powerful than the living
As long as we are alive people don't get scared of us
The moment we die, they get petrified even at the sight of our shadow
Since we are sometimes supposed to turn into ghosts
We become the object of horror people can hardly face
Interestingly, shadows are more powerful than subjects,
Because they are the one to define the existence
They are supple, pliant, resilient and permeable
Mongols are, even today, opposed to the idea of locating the grave of
Genghis Khan
Lest he should unleash something ominous
Even powerful countries are afraid to hear the name of Yasukuni shrine -
a Japanese war memorial, commemorating more than two million dead
Death, a naked representation of Truth, is a direct challenge to the ego
on which is built our mundane persona
Therefore, we fear everything relating to death

# WHO IS NOT AFRAID OF IT?

I am afraid to look at my photographs
They have an aversion to telling a lie
They always tell the Truth
Truth is discourteous, and
Sometimes even frightening
One needs to have courage
To face the Truth
Death is the absolute Truth
Who is not afraid of it?

# TIME'S INSANITY

We are all victims of Time's insanity
It does not know how to honor our feelings
Neither does it know to keep its own promises
It is as dry as the desert, and as cold as death
It is completely unrestrained
It always tries to strip us bare
It enjoys toying with our destiny

# EVERY WEEK I GO TO THE LAUNDRY

Every week I go to the laundry to wash my clothes
I wash my clothes with a blend of soap and bleach
After spending some time at the laundry I come back with clean clothes
When I wear them I find myself vibrant and cheerful
Similarly, every week I go to the temple
I go there in the hope of cleaning my Self
I pay homage to Gods and Goddesses, although they are not on
speaking terms with humans
It is really surprising that I can't help going there
But I have never returned from the temple with the same vibrancy and
cheerfulness as I have from the laundry
Perhaps it might be because the soap and bleach I use there are not that pure
Instead of cleaning, they tend to contaminate my Self
A blend of ego and desire - they cannot whiten my Being
The cleaning machine of the temple seems highly sophisticated
It is so sensitive that it can instantly identify unwanted foreign objects
It promptly rejects them
But we are still so obsessively conditioned that we can hardly morph into
what fits the temple mechanism

# MONARCHY'S AGONY

The moment you rise
I collapse,
Because I cannot withstand you
I am a paralyzed mountain
My height is shrinking, and
Majesty waning
I am anticipating the moment
When I will be turned into a fossil

# I DON'T MIND

I don't mind
If you forget me

I don't mind if
You behave as if
You never knew me

I don't mind
If you choose
Even to incommode me

I will certainly mind
Should my memory
Try to obscure the moments
We shared together

# IN MY DREAM

It has been long
Since I haven't seen you
In my dream

It could be because
You don't want to
Cherish my love

I wish I could
See you in my dream
Not because
I want you to love me

I just want to ensure
That my love toward you
Will never exhaust

# I CANNOT REMAIN CONTENT

I have found you in the beauty of Nature
I have found you in the fragrance of flower
I have found you in the music of stream
But I cannot remain content unless
I find you within my own heart

# ROMEO AND JULIET

Poignant saga of Romeo and Juliet
A land of cactus with obnoxious thorns
Desires are crucified, and passions impaled
Bemoaning souls overwhelmed by the blood, oozing out of love
Time's celebrated pedigree spoilt by the imploding coherence of creation
Stygian darkness permeating the vision of civilization
Oceans are formed with tears of Orpheus
Eurydice is seen no more on earth

# I LIKE BLACK THE MOST

Among colors, I like Black the most
To me, it is the symbol of boldness, chivalry and resistance
Black is the only color with the courage to challenge the white
It also symbolizes darkness
Nothing but darkness can stand up to light
Light must owe its existence to darkness,
Because in the absence of dark, there is no light
Can you imagine anything in this universe without a shadow, a synonym for dark?
Nothing can exist without its support
Were it not for the night, mornings would not have been born
They bring us enormous hopes and optimism, inherited from the calm and tranquility of night
Night is the meditative state of Time
Entire strength of the universe is unleashed through its austerity and contemplation
Black is the counterpoise -
A symbol of negativity that represents the motivating force behind the effervescence of everything positive

# A MESMERIZING FEAT

Life is not only a mosaic of sweet melodies
It is also a receptacle of disconcerting experiences
It could also be a gorgeous source through which flow numerous
streams of love and kindness
While spurned, it can also turn out to be a livid witch, muttering series
of imprecations
Life, a long compound sentence, punctuated by plenty of commas and
semi colons
It wields the potential of transcending full stops
It does not pursue the rules of grammar
Instead, it creates grammars, and gives meaning to our intrinsic
vibrations
Life is something as well as nothing
Really, a mesmerizing feat of a wily magician who himself happens to be
a wondrous creation of magic

# A SENSUAL PANG

When
A woman
Smiles
In the beauty
Of flowers
Nature
Suffers
A sensual pang

# I HAVE NEVER SEEN MYSELF

I have seen lush valleys
I have seen barren lands
I have seen the beauty of Nature
I have seen enchanting smiles
But I have never seen myself
O God, would you please help me remove the veil
That has separated me from my Soul,
The mirror in which I can see myself?

# POEMS ARE SPONTANEOUS OUTBURSTS

Poems are but spontaneous outbursts of a poignant heart
An open sky is their beauty
Just like pervasive spirit they cannot be confined to any boundary
They cry in our anguish, and rejoice in our happiness
They are the frolicking of a stream, and tranquility of vast oceans
Scorching heat of deserts add to their piquancy, and the moonlight to
their solemnity
They sometimes embody the sadistic lust of graves, cemeteries and
necropolis, the only safe havens for humans
They sing in the melody of prayers, reverberating around temples and
churches
They heave a sigh in tribulations of the oppressed and dispossessed
They sing praise for the brave who don't kill but die for humanity
In the realm of poetry, cactus is treated at par with roses,
Because beauty is beautiful no matter how ugly it is
Deserts can turn into verdant land if they perspire at Nature's agony

# CONQUERING THE COSMOS

Butterflies
Fluttering their wings
Tried to encourage me
To scale the grandeur of cosmos

My body, as it was
Tied to the gravity of earth,
Was reluctant
Even to levitate an inch

Butterflies
In apparent exasperation, said -
Conquering the cosmos
Seems beyond your reach

# LEFT IN THE LURCH

Leaves
Wizened, haggard and exhausted
Devoid of tree's protection
Get swayed by cruel wind

Estrangement,
Excruciatingly agonizing
Leaves stare at the face of their mother
Mother tortured at her own helplessness

Impetuous wind
As if livid at leaves' reluctance
Shouts, screams and yells
Ruthlessness knows no bounds

Unable to resist and revolt
Leaves comply with
The wind's byzantine whims
Only to be left in the lurch

# INSOMNIAC EYES

Insomniac eyes,
Longing for rest,
Conjure up images of
Rambha, Tilottama and Urbashi
Performing aerobics

Splendid mix of vivacity and panache,
Exuding transcendental amorousness
Tumescent rivers start flooding
Across my body
Ecstasy ejaculated

# NONE TO CONSOLE

Night with its heart broken
Started weeping,
But
There was none to console
Except my trauma

# O LONELINESS!

O loneliness!
Why do you torture me?
I don't think
I have done any harm to you

O loneliness!
Why do you ridicule me?
I don't think
I have disrespected you

O loneliness!
Why do you agonize me?
I don't think
I have inflicted you

O loneliness!
Why do you jeer at me?
I don't think
I have made fun of you

# O PARAGON OF BEAUTY!

I am completely mesmerized by the streak of smile, embellishing your face
Entire beauty of universe seems hidden behind your eyes
Nothing aesthetic can match the intoxication of your lips
Just as dark clouds bedeck the summer sky, so does the long and black hair add to your elegance
Even a subtle desire for flirtation has convulsed the ocean of my passion that had remained dormant for centuries
O paragon of beauty!
You are the only one who can quench my eternal thirst
But I don't know whether the wind has whispered my yearning unto your ears

# HOUSE FOR RENT

My house is for rent
Anybody can rent it
Honestly speaking, there are some problems
Whoever resides in this house should dare encounter these obstacles:
It is heavily infected by cockroaches
Most of the time it is reigned by rodents
There is no water in the tap
Heating system is out of order
Nosey neighbors never let you live in peace
Despite all these problems, if anybody is really interested,
Please feel free to give me a call

# SPIRIT OF SINCERE EMPATHY

I have never seen God
Neither do I expect to see Him
Except in true love and affection
Moksha, nirvana and deliverance
Are nothing but a state of mind
Wherein we integrate ourselves
With our fellow humans
In a spirit of sincere empathy

# HISTORY IS REPLETE

History is replete with paeans of those
Who possess exceptional caliber of
Writing their destiny with
Blood and tears of the innocent
Rest are mere guinea pigs
In the lab of fate's insanity

# AN ODE TO TIME

Time seems
Dissolving in its
Own silence

I am always
Desperate to steal the
Silence of Time

In silence
Time has found a
Perfect companion

Silence of Time
Is abuzz with unending
Series of revulsions

Isn't death an
Immersion into the
Silence of Time?

From behind
The screen of silence
Time wreaks havoc

Married to
Silence, Time procreates
Cacophony

Hidden behind the
Silence of Time are myriads
Of revolutions

Time often
Impersonates the
Supreme Self

# FLEETING ILLUSION

Normally I am detached
But I don't know why I am so much attached to you
Normally I don't care about anything
But I don't know why I do care so much about you
Normally I don't cry
But I don't know why my heart gets so much lachrymose when I think
of you
O my fellow beings!
Is it that penance, renunciation, detachment, altruism, asceticism and
sacrifice are mere fleeting illusion?
Or the earthly attributes of my persona, true definition of something
divine?

# HUMAN BLOOD

Scientists say human blood is made of RBC and WBC
Please forgive me, I don't believe that
To me, it is made of literature and philosophy, politics and religion
Were it not so, why would they be prepared to die for their identity -
Seemingly abstract and amorphous?

# IGNORE ME

Ignore me, ridicule me, downplay me, disparage me
I don't care even if the world pours its entire venom unto me
I don't care even if the atmosphere disfavors me
I don't care even if my luck choses to jettison me
I don't care even if someone thinks that I am babbling gibberish
My faith and conviction constantly reassures me:
The day will come when the zeitgeist of human psyche will be
reverberated with my message
The celebrated message of 'universality of spirit'
With exceptionally rare intuition, clairvoyance, transport and profundity
Maybe after years, decades or even centuries
Since my words are the pristine echo of my Soul, they represent
mankind's true aspirations that have always inspired them to conquer
the realm of the unknown

# WHAT IS LIFE IF NOT ...

What is life?
If not an urge
For illumination

What is death?
If not a journey
Into the unknown

What is beauty?
If not a penchant
For knowing oneself

What is space?
If not the vastitude
Of one's Self

What is love?
If not a desire to see
Oneself in others

# I LOVED EVERYONE

Destiny once overheard
Human mumbling in
Wistful agony

"Ever since I came to this earth
I loved everyone,
I encountered

"Much to my dismay and despondence,
I have never found anyone
Who has ever loved me

"From day one,
I loved this earth,
I loved this universe

"I loved many things
That I didn't even see

"I know, nobody will shed tears
Over my departure

"I don't believe,
Even my own body will
Choose to mourn my demise

"Stoic and unmoved,
It will instantly start negotiating
Its union with soil

"I have to continue my journey alone"

No sooner had human finished his murmur
Than the lightning flashed out of black clouds

It seemed as if it were a streak of smile - crossing
The face of Destiny - rather sneering and sardonic

# I FIND YOU EVERYWHERE

I find you everywhere;
In the sun, in the moon,
In stars and in deep oceans

I find you in my nerves,
In veins, and in the
Undulating landscape of my psyche

It is perhaps
Just because of your presence
That I find my blood
Predisposed to transgressions

Obstinate and deviant,
My blood is prepared to listen
Neither to my brain,
Nor to my heart

I believe, you are the one
Who is responsible for making
My blood a dissolute tyrant

# THIRST FOR LOVE

My thirst for love
Cannot be quenched
By the smell of flowers,
Neither can their beauty
Gratify my Self

I find myself
In the midst of a desert
That has been widowed
From time immemorial

With all its tears exhausted
Over millions of years,
The desert can neither cry nor weep

Eternal heat of its trauma
Has rendered it dry and harsh
In the same way as
I have been overwhelmed
By agonizing emotions

I have turned into a naked statue, forced
To endure silently onslaughts of Time

# LIFE IS MESMERIZING

I am a nondescript traveler
Suffering from amnesia

Devoid of any background -
Racial, religious, and ethnic -
I have already lost my past

Probably strewn with
Unconscionable afflictions,
Future sometimes sounds to me
Shallow and nebulous

I know nothing about the present,
Except that I myself am present

I carry a colossal universe
Enveloped by my morbid presence

Although exhausted by
The labyrinthine complexities
Of life, I can't help appreciating it

Life is mesmerizing

# SOME HAIKUS

Wrapped in her
Own beauty, Nature
Enthralls us all

Gentle rustling
Of foliage invokes
The whisper of my Soul

Singing of birds
Enraptures me
Enchanting verdure

Diaphanous clouds
Intent on wrapping Moon
In an amorous embrace

The Supreme Being
Meditates unto itself
Creation of the universe

Successive upheavals
In the divine world
Evolution of humans

Solemnity of oceans
Inspires humans to realize
Their own Being

Human though
An insignificant mass,
Wields cosmic power

Vast cosmos
Constantly revolves
Around brain of humans

Insatiable lust
Of bumblebee arousing
Flowers' erotic impulse

Beauty of flowers
Lies in their enigmatic smile
Mona Lisa

Somewhere deep in
Heart resides your Self -
Radiant, eternal and infinite

Incipient rays of sun
With their warm touch
Arouse hope and optimism

Life with millions of
Questions challenges
Our ingenuity

It is the divinity within
Us from which ensue
Love and compassion

Shrouded in superstition
Religion morphs into something -
Callous, brutal and macabre

God did not
Create us, rather
We created Him

Religions commit
Suicide at the altar of
Extremism

May
Each step of mine
Lead to fullness

Diaphanous clouds
Prone to evaporation
Enigma of life

Life and death
Two ends of the spectrum
Listless pendulum

Belief in oneself
Sole message of God
We are God

Each human is God
Unto himself
Revelation of Scriptures

Beautiful flowers
In the garden
Attachment to my wife

Life and death
Two naked realities
Divinity unfolds itself

Small butterflies
Fluttering their wings
Emotion in the high

A Hindu temple
Priests chanting hymns
Solemnity on the wane

Music
A tender appreciation
Heart is pierced

Dew
In the blade of grass
Tears of humanity

Love
Dissolution of ego
Smile of the Supreme

Envy
Poison in psyche
Erosion of Soul

Reading books
An exhilarating experience
Orgasmic ecstasy

Compassion
Buddha's enlightenment
Eternal illusion

Non-violence
An incessant quest
Crying in wilderness

A cactus
In the midst of a desert
Challenges galore

The crown
Symbol of superciliousness
Evanescence

A clock
Hanging on the wall
Life is ephemeral

Kings and emperors
Arrogance knows no bounds
Destiny feels ashamed

The child cries
Mother caresses
It starts drizzling

Powers rise and fall
Nobody bothers to care
Rubbish of history

I dream
Of being a monarch
The snow melts away

I look at stars
They just twinkle
Accelerated heartbeat

Rivers flow and flow
And flow ...
Life never ends

Tradition persists
Time revolts
Metamorphosis

Grave
A gruesome imagery
Earthquake hits the city

Buddha
Humanity redefined
Religion imprisoned

Abraham Lincoln
A bird is set free
Freedom exalted

Karl Marx
Crackling of chains
Ants start swarming

Mao Tse Tung
Reinstatement of order
Freedom incarcerated

Adolf Hitler
Horror horrified at
Its horridness

Life is a journey
Full of dichotomies
Earth goes round the sun

Medicine
Date expired
Hope evaporates

A child
With a pen in hand
Everything is predestined

Love is an art
Its subtlety enraptures
Communion of two souls

Puppets are dancing
Someone pulls the string
Life is uncertain

Writing is a pleasure
It is an endless quest
Truth seems elusive

Horses gallop
They measure the earth
Moon is too far

Ideals survive
Despite being bruised
The earth is round

Solitude
It is too frightening
Myriads of stars in the sky

It is raining
The universe is drenched
Tears in the eyes of future

Life in exile
An agonizing experience
Light at the end of tunnel

Arrogance and compassion
Cannot go hand in hand
Darkness devours light

A peep into the past
Gives nostalgic exhilaration
Life is but transient

A plane takes off
As soon as passengers board
Unpredictable future

Since long
My watch is broken
Time is mum

With emotions restrained
One can realize the Supreme
Transcendental illusion

A glass of Coke
Cannot quench my thirst
Insatiate sand

Alone, all alone
Time is not running fast
Dark clouds in the sky

Seeing someone
Naked is exciting
Sounds immoral

Once in power
Makes one feel supreme
Power is but transient

Scriptures are
Sublime echo of
Our divine Self

Love
An enigmatic contraption
Blushing Moon

O my tears,
Why do you want
To reveal yourself?

How poignant
My tears are, just
Let them hide!

Let agony
Speak through tears
Morning dew

Beauty blushes
From behind the veil
Diaphanous clouds

Try to reduce
Yourself to abstraction
$E=mc2$

Life is a puzzle
We're engaged in fixing it
Arctic crevices

Fire and fury
A befitting rhetoric
Volcanic eruption

Malice towards none
Something alien to our psyche
Oppositional politics

Distortion of truth
Impaired cognitive response
Expanding soil erosion

Who are you
To define what poetry is?
Infinite are Time and Space

I can see
The face of present
Born out of past

I often get lost
In the dream of Time
Apocalypse

Starry sky
Stirs up my passion
Sweet fragrance

Devotion is
A desire to flirt with
Providence

The moment
I get lost in void
I become full

The path always
Walks ahead of me
Egomania

What is the
Relation between me
And my shadow?

Someone waves
The baton, and we
Start dancing

Give me a piece
Of chalk, I'll give you
A civilization

From the depth
Of our conscience comes
The voice of God

Bigotry and fanaticism
Extremism and radicalism
Death and destruction

Simple definition
Of life - a path leading
To nothingness

Silhouettes of camels
Ambling in a vast desert
Full moon

Having their
Tears all dried up, deserts
Suffer scorching heat

Dinosaurs became
Extinct, do we also
Face the same fate?

Birds flying in
The blue sky don't
Suffer acrophobia

You will not die
Even after your death
Eternal verity

Perhaps in search
Of its shadow sunlight
Comes down to earth

From the window
Of our deeds fate peeps
Into our future

Your face in
The mirror echoes the
Caveat of Time

In the distant
Horizon I see the rainbow
Of my future

I don't know
Why my shadow
Doesn't speak to me

O my shadow,
Why do you desert me
Once I fall?

Have you ever seen
Light submit to the
Sovereignty of dark?

I am in
The universe
Universe I am

I am lost
In my Self
Still I am

Even in death's
Howl I can hear
Music of life

What is death?
If not an eternal
Loss of memory

Agony
Cherishes the company
Of tears

Oceans, infatuated
By the beauty of Moon,
Rise to embrace it

Stars can't stand the
The beauty of Moon,
And hide behind the dark

Blushing Moon hides
Behind the veil of clouds
Amorous palpitation

Although two faces
Of the same Truth, why can't
Light and Dark coexist?

Will Kingdom of God
Ever be established on earth?
Eternal hallucination

Is God really
Thirsty for our
Obsequiousness?

Our imaginations
Mimic undulating waves
Of vast oceans

Where shall I seek
God, in the universe or
In my own Self?

Why can't man
Dare rise above
Gods and deities?

To whom does
Wind owe its impetuosity?
Galaxies collide

Will the Creator
Ever try to understand
Our sufferings?

Is Buddha a product
Of disease, old age and death?
Ever-gasping nirvana

Tyranny is rooted
In our readiness to submit
Talons of a hawk

How long is
The journey of man,
Does it ever end?

What makes
Sky blush in
The morning?

Water morphs
Into ice to revolt against
Nature's tyranny

I see pearl like
Dew drops illuminating
The Leaves of Grass

Freedom comes more
From your blood than
From the Constitution

One cannot
Inherit liberty, it
Has to be earned

Freedom and
Liberty outweigh the worth
Of your life

Let courage
And boldness define
Your existence

Tyranny
Thrives in your
Submission

Spew fire
Burn tyranny
To ashes

Explore the
Enormous power
Hidden within

Left alone by
Leaves, trees seek
Mercy of Time

It is the height of
Life that counts more
Than its length

It takes enormous moxie
To question one's
Own belief

God lies in
Your belief, not the
Other way around

God is the cheapest
Object ever sold in
Human market

Courage
You can't buy
In market

Nothing's greater
Than the greatness
Of the great

Truth is the
Most lethal among
Explosives

# NOTES

## Mea Culpa

p. xv  Vishwaroop
Universal form of Lord Krishna, as described in the Bhagavadgita.

p. xvii  Aham Brahmashmi
I am Brahma, the Absolute Reality. It is one of the four Grand Pronouncements of the Vedas.

## America Arise And Awake

p. 1  kundalini
According to Hinduism, a kind of extraordinary divine energy, located in human spine.

p. 4  Klaibyam masmagama
Uttishthata, jagrata
Yield not to unmanliness. (Bhagavadgita 2/3)
Arise and awake. (Katha Upanishad 1/3/14)

p. 5  Atma and paramatma
Soul and Super Soul.

p. 7  Ayam atma brahma
This Soul is God. It is one of the four Grand Pronouncements of the Vedas.

p. 12  Brahmaiva tena gantabyam
Certainly the Supreme Reality is achievable. (Bhagavadgita 4/24)

p. 16  Pandavas and Kauravas at Kurukshetra
Two major clans who had fought each other at Kurukshetra, India, during the war of the Mahabharata.

p. 25  Prakriti, gunas – satwa, rajas and tamas
Hinduism refers to Prakriti as the primal material energy. Guna is its innate character, comprising of three attributes purity, activity and darkness. It is believed that the interplay between these three forces is responsible for the manifestation of the universe.

p. 27  Bibhishan
Bibhishan who betrayed his brother Ravana, the King of Lanka, and cooperated with the latter's enemy, Rama, the legendary hero of the Ramayana.

p. 31  gopikas
Maiden unmarried girls with whom Lord Krishna used to have raasleela.

p. 34  yogah karmasu kaushalam
Yoga is excellence at work. (Bhagavadgita 2/50)

p. 34  raaga, bhaya and krodha
Desire, fear and anger.

p. 35  Yajnavalkya, Janak, Nachiketa, Barun, Uddalaka and Angiras
Reverential seers, sages and philosophers of the East.

p. 36  prana
In Hindu literature, prana is described as 'life force' that also tends to carry deep philosophical overtone.

p. 37  Arjuna
The great hero of the Mahabharata.

**Beauty Of Nature**

p. 72  Satyam, Shivam and Sundaram
Truth, Godliness and Beauty.

**I Wonder ...**

p. 79  Shantanu, Bhishma, Parasar, Satyavati, Shuktimati, Vasu, Kolahala
Different characters mentioned in the epic, Mahabharata.

**O Callous Murderer Of Damascus**

p. 90  Kamsa, Yogmaya
Kamsa is the maternal uncle of Lord Krishna. Kamsa who wanted to kill
Krishna as soon as he was born, was warned by Yogmaya, the eight-handed
Goddess, that the child who would kill him had already been born in
Gokul.

**What An Irony, Indeed!**

p. 93  Dharmaraj Yudhisthir
He was the eldest among the five Pandavas, who won the Mahabharata
war. Yudhisthir was believed to be the embodiment of truth, justice and
righteousness.

p. 93  Yama
God of Death in Hinduism.

**Pyongyang Is Desperate**

p. 102  Kurmavatar, Nrisinghavatar, Barahavatar, Ramavatar
The giant tortoise, the half man-half lion, Rama, the hero of the epic,
Ramayana. According to Hindu mythology, they are all believed to be the
reincarnations of Lord Bishnu, born in this world to destroy the enemies
of truth, justice and righteousness.

p. 102  Raudraroop
One of the features of Lord Shiva that depicts him extremely apoplectic.

**Nature Intoxicated**

p. 134  charu
Offering.

p. 134  Om Shantih, Dhyouh Shantih, Prithvi Shantih, Aapah Shantih
May there be peace in heaven. May there be peace in the sky. May there be peace in the earth. May there be peace in the water. These are the sacred mantras of the Vedas.

**Why Not Find Some Better Alternative?**

p. 162  Kalpa
A great length of time in Sanskrit language.

**How Can I Believe?**

p. 197  Narad
One of the most celebrated sages of Hindu mythologies. He always used to wander from place to place with the message of enlightening wisdom.

**Let Me Revel**

p. 203  Lila
Divine play between the Absolute and the phenomenal world.

**A Dream, Horrid And Surreal**

p. 238  Sudarshan Chakra
An extraordinarily powerful disc-like weapon Lord Krishna used to wield.

p. 239  Naasato vidyate bhaavo naabhaavo vidyate satah
Never has the unreal any existence, and the real never ceases to be. (Bhagavadgita 2/16)

## I Preach Revolution

p. 248  Charvaka
One of the earliest Indian school of thoughts that rejected the basic foundation of the Vedas, and accompanying rituals.

p. 248  Sarbadharman parityajya mamekam sharanam braja
Surrendering your entire duties unto Me, take refuge in Me alone. (Bhagavadgita 18/66)

## I Feel Like Drinking The Moon

p. 258  jyotirlinga
The pillar of radiance representing the omnipotence of Lord Shiva.

## Time Would Have Mourned

p. 282  Mahabhinishkramana
Great Renunciation of Siddhartha, who later became the Buddha.

## Insomniac Eyes

p. 300  Rambha, Tilottama and Urbashi
Divine beauties of heaven, often described as the most captivating enchantresses in Hindu mythologies.

Printed in the United States
By Bookmasters